DEAD COMPANIES WALKING

DEAD COMPANIES WALKING

HOW A HEDGE FUND MANAGER FINDS OPPORTUNITY IN UNEXPECTED PLACES

SCOTT FEARON

WITH

JESSE POWELL

St. Martin's Press

New York

www.stmartins.com

Designed by Letra Libre, Inc.

Library of Congress Cataloging-in-Publication Data

Fearon, Scott.
    Dead companies walking : how a hedge fund manager finds opportunity in unexpected places / Scott Fearon.
        pages   cm
    Includes bibliographical references.
    ISBN 978-1-137-27964-4 (hardcover)
    ISBN 978-1-4668-7920-1 (ebook)
    1. Short selling. 2. Speculation. 3. Success in business. I. Title.
    HG6041.F38 2015
    332.63'228—dc23

                                                    2014020146

Our books may be purchased in bulk for promotional, educational, or business use. Please contact your local bookseller or the Macmillan Corporate and Premium Sales Department at 1-800-221-7945, extension 5442, or by email at MacmillanSpecialMarkets@macmillan.com.

First published by Palgrave Macmillan, a division of St. Martin's Press LLC

First St. Martin's Press Edition: January 2015

10   9   8   7   6   5   4   3

Dedicated to everyone who
loves, educates, worries about, and cares for
intellectually and physically disabled
children and adults.
You are selfless, unsung heroes.

CONTENTS

FORGED IN FAILURE

If you want to increase your success rate, double your failure rate.

—Thomas J. Watson

If you don't know who you are, the stock market is an expensive place to find out.

—George Goodman, aka Adam Smith

LIKE A LOT OF QUINTESSENTIALLY AMERICAN STORIES, MY career in money management began with a road trip. It was the summer of 1983. I'd just graduated from business school in leafy Evanston, Illinois, and landed my first job at the largest bank in Texas. On a clear, breezy summer morning, I piled three suitcases' worth of my belongings into the trunk of my powder blue Oldsmobile Delta 88 and headed for the bank's headquarters in Houston. I was eager to start my new life as a financial executive. The economy of Texas was riding a ten-year boom. A barrel of light sweet crude was going for over thirty bucks, three times more than in the mid-1970s, and just about everyone expected it to go a whole lot higher.

Little did I know, as I tooled down Highway 57, I was actually driving toward a catastrophe. A Category Five economic hurricane was brewing off the coast of Houston, and it hit shortly after I arrived in town. The price of oil began to fall. Then, in January 1986, Saudi Arabia opened the spigots and swamped the market with cheap crude. In a single day, oil crashed below $10 a barrel, and the entire economy of Texas imploded. Scores of energy companies went bankrupt. Unemployment shot up. "For Sale" signs swung in the yards of abandoned houses. Vast asphalt parking lots sat vacant in front of shuttered department stores. Entire neighborhoods turned into ghost towns.

Just like that, my budding career seemed to be over before it started. The bank immediately froze my $30,000-a-year salary, and every morning I came in to work expecting to find a pink slip pinned to the wall of my cubicle.

If this sounds familiar, it should. It was a small, regional preview of the global meltdown that came in the wake of the 2008 financial crisis. But for those of us who were in East Texas in the 1980s, it didn't seem small or regional. It was cataclysmic—and it shaped me as an individual, a businessperson, and an investor. What I didn't realize at the time was that living through that bust was the luckiest thing that would ever happen to me. It taught me perhaps the single most important lesson about business and about life: *Things go wrong more often than they go right.* Failure is actually a natural—even crucial—element of a healthy economy. And the people who are willing to acknowledge that fact can make a hell of a lot of money.

THE BUSINESS OF FAILURE

Shortly after the collapse, I left Houston for the San Francisco Bay Area. From 1987 to 1990, I managed a mutual fund in downtown San Francisco. Since 1991, I've run a hedge fund from a modest Marin County office park in the shadow of Mount Tamalpais. I've lived through several more booms and busts since then, but I've almost always managed to make a profit, even in the worst of times. Over twenty-three years, my fund rose roughly 1,100 percent after all fees—significantly higher than the S&P 500's total return during that same period. I credit one thing above all for this success. *Long ago, I learned to appreciate one of the most enduring and important American business traditions: failure.*

While most of my fund's investments are in the stocks of companies I believe are undervalued, I also look for stocks that are *over*valued by the markets. My specialty is identifying what I call "dead companies walking"— businesses on their way to bankruptcy and a zeroed-out share price. To the noninvestor, earning money on losing stocks might sound counterintuitive. But short selling is a routine, if widely misunderstood, investment strategy. And while it may seem macabre to profit on the misfortunes of others, investors like me make our markets stronger and more efficient.

We Americans like to think we have the greatest economy in the history of the world. And we do. But most people don't really understand why. It's not just because of our plentiful natural resources or our global dominance or our business-friendly politics. It's because, until recently anyway, we have allowed ourselves and our markets an unprecedented amount of freedom—not only the freedom to grow and make obscenely large profits, but also the freedom to fall flat on our faces.

As paradoxical as it seems, thriving, dynamic market economies—like ours has been for most of its history—embrace failure. In contrast, economies that try to manage failure by propping up slumping businesses lag behind because they don't grow or innovate. Japan is probably the best recent example of this phenomenon. The country is notorious for keeping moribund but politically favored corporations alive, and the results of that strategy are plain. It has been mired in a zero-growth economy since I first tried sushi in the late 1980s.

I spend a good deal of time visiting and studying companies in Silicon Valley. That place has taken on an almost mythical status in the business world, and deservedly so. It's chock-full of smart, creative people. Without all the high-tech innovations they've come up with in the last half century, the global economy would be dead in the water. But no one talks about the real reason the Valley is such fertile ground: failure. It's the biggest, most volatile petri dish of raw capitalism on the planet. New ideas and companies are put to the test rapidly and ruthlessly. The good ones survive. The bad ones don't. Sure, they might get some buzz and even some big initial funding. But if they don't have what it takes, they die a quick death. Even when the region is doing well, dozens of unheralded companies come on the scene every year, only to fade away.

The Austrian economist Joseph Schumpeter called this process "creative destruction." It's a harsh but vital process. It weeds out subpar ideas and gives good ones like Google the nourishment they need to grow. Short-sellers help make this happen. We identify the duds, which is good not only for the larger economy but also for the people involved in those ventures. Even the smartest people can get caught up in bad ideas or bad ways of doing business. The sooner they are disabused of these flawed practices, the better for everyone.

NOTHING SPECIAL

The money manager David Rocker identified three types of businesses that falter and go under: "frauds, fads, and failures."* The frauds—like WorldCom and Enron—get most of the attention, because their stories are usually dramatic, full of intrigue and greed and deception. But frauds are an infinitesimal fraction of the number of companies that fail every year. Fads—companies or products that explode onto the scene before fizzling out, like Pac-Man and the Hula Hoop—are also relatively rare. Most companies that enter bankruptcy fall into the third category. They're just plain old failures, the result of bad ideas, bad management, or a combination of the two.

As the manager of my hedge fund, I've shorted the stocks of over two hundred companies that have eventually gone bankrupt. Many of these businesses started out with promising, even inspired ideas: natural cures for common diseases, for example, or a cool new kind of sporting goods product. Others were once-thriving organizations trying to rebound from hard times. Despite their differences, *they all failed because their leaders made one or more of six common mistakes that I look for:*

1. They learned from only the recent past.
2. They relied too heavily on a formula for success.
3. They misread or alienated their customers.
4. They fell victim to a mania.
5. They failed to adapt to tectonic shifts in their industries.

---

*David Rocker, "The Short Perspective in Today's Markets," *CFA Institute Conference Proceedings Quarterly,* June 2005.

6. They were physically or emotionally removed from their companies' operations.

I will describe each of these six deadly business sins in the following chapters and give several examples of each from my three decades of observing both failing and successful companies. As you'll see, I've committed a number of these sins myself as both an investor and a businessperson. In addition to running my fund, I've opened two restaurants. My second attempt in that notoriously failure-prone industry has been very successful; my first closed in less than three years. That's right—I have personally run a dead company walking.

I'd like to think my recollections can help corporate leaders and investors avoid these same mistakes. However, I didn't set out to write a simple how-to, or maybe how-*not*-to, guide for management and investing. I hope this book can accomplish something more. It might sound strange, but I want to *celebrate* failure, or at least take away some of its stigma.

In my experience, the vast majority of people who fail in business are neither idiots for believing in their companies nor swindlers looking to dupe their customers and investors. All of the executives I am going to describe, even the ones who suffered the worst disasters, were intelligent, honest, and hard-working individuals. I have a great deal of respect for anyone who tries and fails in business, and I hope that when you finish this book, you will recognize just how ordinary, and important, failure is. It's a critical part of what makes a healthy market economy—and it happens every day to some of the smartest people in the world.

ONE

HISTORICAL MYOPIA

"How did you go bankrupt?" Bill asked.
"Two ways," Mike said. "Gradually and then suddenly."

—Ernest Hemingway, *The Sun Also Rises*

A MAN NAMED GEOFF RAYMOND TAUGHT ME THE BASICS of money management. He ran the investment division at Texas Commerce Bank in Houston. But Geoff was far from your average straight-laced banker. He wore his flowing blond hair down past his ears. He favored pastel shirts with white collars and gold or silver collar bars. And he was the fastest walker I've ever seen. Anytime we went anywhere by foot, I almost had to jog to keep up with him. He told me he'd learned to speed walk like that during his days working at Citibank in Lower Manhattan. He'd figured out that if you walked like Carl Lewis ran, you could make every green light heading uptown. But when it came to picking stocks, Geoff was never in a hurry. He was very deliberate. And he believed in something extremely unusual in those days—actual research.

More than anything—more than projections and book values and price-to-earnings ratios—Geoff believed human-to-human contact was the best way to gauge a company's future performance. He valued numbers and raw data, but he knew that numbers were easy to fudge or misread. You had to study the people behind the numbers to get the full story. And reading secondhand profiles about a company's executives didn't count. Neither did pressing their flesh and swapping a few jokes with them at an investor conference. You had to go see them where they lived and worked—their own offices.

The very first company I brought to Geoff as a potential investment for Texas Commerce's trust accounts was called Global Marine (stock symbol: GLM). The company owned a fleet of offshore drilling rigs and ships that it would lease out to oil companies. Ten years before I came to Houston, it also got into a funny side business when its former owner, Howard Hughes, built a giant ship named the *Glomar Explorer* and leased it to the CIA to help salvage a wrecked Soviet submarine out in the middle of the Pacific Ocean. Like just about every other energy-related outfit in Texas, Global Marine had gotten very rich during the oil boom. And even though its stock price was at a multiyear low in 1984, around $5, the company still had a lot of assets. Its book value—assets minus liabilities divided by total shares outstanding—was around $10. That meant, by classic value investment standards, GLM was a potential winner. I grabbed my handmade earnings models and proudly strolled into Geoff's office.

"This looks good, Scott," he said. "Let's go pay them a visit and see what they have to say."

I MADE A CALL TO GLOBAL MARINE'S CORPORATE OFFICE and arranged a meeting with the company's chief financial officer, a man named Jerry.* The next morning I found myself jogging through the bank's parking garage, trying to keep up with Geoff. We took my Oldsmobile about twenty miles west on the Katy Freeway, as I-10 is known in Houston, until we reached Global Marine's six-story, glass-fronted headquarters off Memorial Drive. It was late in the summer, the hottest, stickiest time of year in East Texas. The temperature was pushing a hundred, and the humidity wasn't far behind. By the time I chased Geoff from the parking lot to the front door of the place, I was gushing sweat.

It wasn't just the heat that was making me perspire. This was the first company visit of my life. I was nervous as hell. And you know what? Even though I've gone on more than 1,400 office visits since then, I still get a little amped up as I head in to meet management teams. It's exciting. You never know what you're going to hear.

Jerry was a polite, friendly, unpretentious guy. He wore a polo shirt and slacks and drank his coffee from a Styrofoam cup. He was also very bullish on Global Marine's future. I wouldn't go so far as to call him cocky. He was too reserved and soft-spoken for that. But he didn't seem the least bit concerned about the fact that the company's stock had taken a virtual nosedive. He had a ready answer for that, and for why we should snap up every GLM share we could find for the bank's accounts.

"The oil business is cyclical by its nature," he said as he sipped at his coffee. "We're down for a little while and then we're up again. Seventy percent. That's the magic number."

"Seventy percent of what?" I asked, mopping my still-moist brow.

---

*I don't think it would be helpful to give Jerry's full name. The same is true for most of the executives I describe in the book. Also, the conversations I recount are based on recollections and notes from my meetings with them.

"Seventy percent utilization, the number of our drilling rigs currently leased out worldwide," he explained. "Right now, we're just below seventy. And that means one thing as far as you guys are concerned: buy, buy, and buy some more. I've been in this business for decades, and 70 percent is always the bottom. It never fails. Look, I'll show you."

He pulled a chart out for me and traced the up-and-down cycle of Global Marine's "rig utilization rate" over the previous few decades. Sure enough, every time the rate slipped below seventy, it turned around and shot up shortly thereafter.

Jerry gave me a self-assured smile. "I'm telling you, Scott. Now's the time to get in."

As we drove back on the Katy Freeway toward Texas Commerce's gleaming headquarters in the distance, Geoff turned to me and said, "Well, what do you think?"

I watched the road for a little while, trying to figure out why I was so reluctant to pull the trigger on GLM. It was a classic winner according to the rules of value investing. The share price was half the company's book value. And Jerry's presentation had been very persuasive. I'm sure most twenty-five-year-old financial rookies—and even a lot of seasoned money managers—would have left Global Marine's offices eager to buy into the company. But I just couldn't.

First, even back then, I knew how risky it was to predict the bottom of a downturn. On Wall Street, they call it "trying to catch a falling knife." Second, I recognized that as accomplished, intelligent, and sincere as Jerry was, he couldn't help but suffer from an unconscious bias in favor of Global Marine. His financial security depended on the company turning around as he was predicting. If he allowed himself to believe that Global Marine was at risk, he wouldn't have been sitting in his office sipping coffee and showing me charts. He would have been out looking for another job.

Given these two concerns, I did the same thing I've done countless times since that humid morning in Houston when confronted with a difficult call on a stock: nothing. Over the years, I've found that doing nothing is often the soundest investment strategy.

"I can't recommend that we buy it," I said to Geoff. "Not yet. I'd rather hold off and get it on the way up, at $7 or even $10. It might cost us a few bucks in profit, but at least we'll be sure that they're going in the right direction."

I expected Geoff to test me more or at least to question my reasoning a little bit. What I was suggesting didn't really mean just "a few bucks in profit." If Jerry's predictions came true and Global Marine's stock took off, the difference between buying in at $5 and $7 or $10 would mean leaving millions on the table. But to my surprise, Geoff just shrugged and said, "Okay. What do you want for lunch?"

I never got the chance to buy GLM on the way up, because it never went up. Like every other company in the Texas oil patch after the price of crude collapsed, Global Marine's stock sank faster than a drilling bit in soft bayou mud. And Jerry's "magic" utilization rate number? It went right down with it. As the oil services industry unraveled, utilization dropped from 70 percent to 25 percent. I don't think the trend line in the chart Jerry showed me in his office even went that low. A share of Global Marine's stock was trading under $1 by mid-1985. In January 1986, less than eighteen months after Jerry urged me to "buy, buy, buy," Global Marine filed for bankruptcy.

I do not believe Jerry was stupid for thinking Global Marine would rebound from its slump. For one thing, he was far from alone. If I gave you a nickel for every person in the energy business in 1984 who believed a big, successful company like Global Marine would go bankrupt within two years, you wouldn't have had enough to afford a gumball. No one, and I mean *no one,* thought things would get as bad as they did.

Nowadays, Dubai is the poster child for petrodollar extravagance, with oil-rich sheiks spending billions on crazy projects like man-made islands and indoor ski resorts in the middle of the Arabian Desert. But trust me, Dubai has nothing on Houston in the early 1980s.* On my first morning living there, I woke up to a loud, hive-like buzz above my apartment near Buffalo Bayou. Half asleep, I walked out onto my balcony and watched dozens of helicopters whirring above the choked freeways of the city. A coworker later told me that a quarter of all privately owned copters in the United States flew over the greater Houston metropolitan area at the time. They were there in such numbers because the city's oilmen all wanted to live like James Dean in the movie *Giant*. They built custom mansions on ranches the size of small nations and rode thirty, forty, even a hundred miles into town every morning by air.

I'll discuss the dangers of getting caught up in manias like the 1980s oil boom later. For now, let's return to Jerry's misguided, but highly instructive, confidence in his magic rig utilization rate number. It's an example of a common mistake I've seen plenty of times over the years.

There is a good reason that Jerry's utilization graph didn't go all the way down to 25 percent—quite simply, it had "never" happened before. I put the word *never* in quotes because I don't mean it literally. And that's the root of the mistake I'm talking about.

---

*Before the price of oil collapsed, there were plans afoot to build the world's tallest building twenty miles west of downtown.

Everybody always stresses the importance of learning from history: "Those who don't learn from the mistakes of the past are doomed to repeat them," the saying goes. In my experience, most people heed this advice, but only up to a point. They study the past quite closely and glean as many lessons from it as they can. But they almost never look back far enough. They confine themselves to the history of the previous few years, or perhaps a decade or two. In other words, it's not that people don't learn from the past. They do—but only the *recent past*. And that can be a deadly error.

I can't remember exactly how far back Jerry's rig utilization chart stretched in time, but it wasn't more than twenty years. Over that time span, Jerry was perfectly right: Global Marine's utilization rate had never stayed below 70 percent for more than a quarter or two. But Jerry assumed that just because the trend had persisted for as long as he could remember, or even a good deal longer, things had *always* been like that. Of course, that was not the case. Looking over a longer period of time, the oil business has suffered numerous catastrophic meltdowns. But because he had never lived through one himself, Jerry—along with everyone else in Houston—didn't even entertain the possibility that the time was ripe for another one.

It's a classic mistake in business and in life. Call it historical myopia. We assume the recent past is the most accurate predictor of the future and that the more distant past is less important or less relevant. Yes, as Jerry pointed out to me, business moves in cycles. The energy sector in particular goes up and down all the time. But those cycles are both large and small. Most cycles run their course over the span of months or years. Others take longer to play out—sometimes much, much longer. But that doesn't mean that those larger, less frequent *supercycles,* as the academics call them, aren't just as regular as the shorter ones. They are. Forgetting that fact has gotten a lot of businesspeople, and investors, in deep trouble. In 2011, scores of textile and apparel companies were crushed when cotton prices suddenly shot up. Nobody in the industry hedged against this kind of supercycle event because, as with the equally steep decline in Global Marine's rig utilization percentage, it had "never" happened before. Of course, in reality, cotton (like oil and steel and every other commodity) has seen numerous large spikes and crashes in the past—*just not in the recent past.* People didn't look back far enough, and it cost them dearly.

Investors also frequently fail to look beyond the recent past and not just by trusting shortsighted corporate executives like Jerry. When I started out at Texas Commerce Bank, I practiced Geoff Raymond's method for picking stocks, called value investing—that is, measuring a company's stock price against its assets, cash flows, dividend yields, and other fundamentals. As I said, that's how I discovered Global Marine as a potential investment. But as my career progressed, I started prioritizing a company's growth outlook over its current value. The reason I began to shy away from value investing was because I noticed that even its most accomplished practitioners often fall victim to historical myopia. They fixate on a company's recent performance or financials while ignoring larger cycles, trends, and secular changes.

In 2007, a powerhouse private equity consortium backed in part by none other than the great Warren Buffett took on a staggering amount of debt to acquire Texas's largest regulated utility, TXU Electric Delivery. At a cool $45 billion, it was the biggest leveraged buyout in history. Thanks to historical myopia, it will probably go down as one of the worst investments ever, too.

LUNCH WITH KEN

One day early in my stay in Houston, I drove across town to a lunch meeting in the Transco Tower. Transco was a pipeline company, and the lunch speaker was the relatively unknown CEO of a company known at the time as Houston Natural Gas. I glanced at the program and nudged the person next to me. "What do you know about this guy, Ken Lay?" I asked him. He shrugged and went back to sawing at his skirt steak.

A short while later, the familiar *whoop-whoop-whoop* of an approaching copter shook the room. We all looked up from our plates in time to see the bird touch down on the helipad next door to the building's conference room. A studious-looking man held his Stetson in place as he deplaned. He made his way into the room and gave an incredibly boring lecture wherein he predicted that energy markets would soon be entirely deregulated. He said that his company, which would be renamed Enron just a short while after this meeting, would one day rival behemoths like IBM and Exxon in revenues.

The guy next to me finished his lunch and immediately nodded off. I desperately wanted to join him, but I fought to keep my eyes open. Lay's soft-spoken delivery didn't come close to matching the grandeur of his predictions. He talked more like a librarian than a budding tycoon. But the rhetoric was not surprising. Before the price of oil collapsed, people were making big, bold—dare I say Texas-sized?—predictions like that all over town. Anything and everything seemed possible.

TXU—renamed Energy Future Holdings Corporation after the deal was consummated—derived a great deal of its revenues by operating coal-fired electricity plants, which it used to supply power to customers in the Dallas metro area. For years leading up to the deal, high electricity prices brought in enormous amounts of free cash flow for TXU, and the company's management planned to build a dozen additional coal-fired plants to generate even more cash. With demand for power rising every year, and electricity prices following suit, TXU appeared to be a value investment gold mine to Buffett and the company's private equity buyers. But by focusing on backward-looking metrics like cash flow and electricity prices, they turned deaf ears to two very loud alarm bells.

First, despite the lobbying efforts of the coal industry (and its oxymoronic promise to create "clean coal" technologies), burning coal is still the dirtiest way to generate power, and the political and social climate is not exactly welcoming to new coal-based electric projects. Even in business-friendly Texas, TXU's plans were quite controversial—and before the acquisition was even finished, the buyout group bowed to pressure from environmental groups and agreed not to build most of the new plants.* But that wasn't the worst thing that happened to the company's new owners. They were so busy salivating over TXU's cash flows that they forgot the lesson Jerry and the rest of the executives at Global Marine had learned several decades earlier—the energy industry is as volatile as a live wire, and expecting short-term results to continue into the future is almost never a safe bet.

---

*Steven Mufson and David Cho, "Energy Firm Accepts $45 Billion Takeover Bid," *Washington Post*, February 26, 2007.

Even as the ink was still drying on the buyout deal, massive new natural gas deposits were being discovered all over North America. As that huge supply of cheaper, cleaner-burning gas came onto the market, electricity prices dropped drastically; TXU's cash flows shrank with them. The only thing that did not shrink was the company's debt load. By 2013, the giant utility was hiring lawyers to handle its impending reorganization.* In 2014, the inevitable finally occurred. The company declared bankruptcy. As for Buffett, he was his usual honest and humble self. He called his decision to purchase $2 billion worth of bonds in Energy Future Holdings' "a major unforced error."†

TXU's implosion was record breaking, but it was hardly unprecedented. When I was still in Texas visiting companies like Global Marine, so-called fern bar chains like TGI Fridays and Bennigan's were all the rage. TGI Fridays even went public in 1983. Its stock sustained a long rally after its initial public offering, mainly because, like TXU, the company generated a tremendous amount of free cash flow. Selling high-margin products always brings in a lot of cash, and there aren't many products with higher margins than cocktails. Value investors got so drunk on those cash flow figures that many of them missed a sobering reality—the company's growth was slowing. For a good while, its stock sold at a small multiple of its cash flow, which meant, by value standards, it was still cheap. But one thing I've learned in this business is that cheap

---

*Mark Chediak, "Oncor Lower Earnings Forecast Cuts Valuation," *Bloomberg News,* October 16, 2013.

†Stephen Grocer, "Warren Buffett Likely Not Going to Like This TXU News," *Wall Street Journal,* February 7, 2013.

can be very expensive, and as the fern bar craze waned, those cash flows went as flat as a bad wine spritzer.

The history of the restaurant industry shows that even popular establishments have to update their menus and decors to survive. Casual fine dining businesses almost always fail if they don't tweak their concepts over time. Even loyal customers get tired of the same old thing, and that was a major problem for fern bars. They were locked into being . . . fern bars. That singular concept was their entire raison d'être, and it was bound to get stale at some point. People who paid attention to TGI Fridays' growth numbers caught the inflection point when the fern bar fad began to subside. The ones who continued to base their decisions on value metrics like multiples of cash flow waited too long to leave the party and got hammered because of it.

TGI Fridays taught me the importance of growth over value investing. It was also the very first stock I shorted. I was studying the company's numbers in my cubicle at Texas Commerce Bank, and I noticed that its revenue growth had begun to shrink over the previous few quarters. It was still making a handsome profit, and it was still trading for a low multiple of its cash flow, but it was opening fewer new bars and earnings growth at its existing locations was tapering off. The end of another quarter was approaching, and on a lark, I opened a personal brokerage account so I could short its stock. Sure enough, its revenues missed expectations and TGI Fridays' share price dropped.

These examples show the danger of learning from only the recent past instead of paying attention to larger, less frequent cyclical patterns. But they're tiny compared to the most disastrous case of historical myopia this country, and maybe the world, has ever seen. The 1980s oil bust, as bad as it was, was largely contained to a single region. The late 2000s real estate crash almost brought down the entire global economy. And it, too, happened because everybody forgot to learn from all of history, not just the history they could remember.

REAR-ENDED

Fast-forward exactly twenty-four years to 2008, in Orange County, California.

I flew into John Wayne Airport and picked up a rental car from the agent at the terminal. It was the middle of January on a beautiful Southern California morning—mid-seventies, clear, and sunny. A pleasant offshore breeze had blown the smog out to sea, leaving the air fresh and clean. To the east, the snowcapped Santa Ana Mountains sparkled in the distance. I climbed into my rented SUV and guided it out of the airport and onto MacArthur Boulevard toward the San Diego Freeway. I checked my watch. I was due to meet executives of a real estate development company called California Coastal Communities (stock symbol: CALC) in a half hour. If there wasn't too much traffic, I would be right on time.

A week earlier, I had targeted Cal Coastal as a potential short investment. It suffered from the two best indicators of a company on its way to bankruptcy—rapidly shrinking revenues and a quickly rising debt load. It's simple economic physics. As revenues go down, debt obligations go up, because companies that are losing money have to take on more debt to pay for things like rent, raw materials, and other overhead expenses. Pretty soon, if they keep losing money, they can't make interest or principal payments to their creditors and they're forced to go into Chapter 11. Many people, even seasoned investors, misunderstand what bankruptcy actually means. They assume that a company shuts its doors forever the day it files and most employees lose their jobs. But that is often not the case. Bankruptcy is fundamentally about reorganizing a firm's *capital structure,* as bondholders and other creditors often agree to ownership stakes in the new incarnation of the company. A lot of businesses emerge from Chapter 11 in better financial shape. (I'll talk later about former Continental Airlines CEO Frank Lorenzo, who actually used bankruptcy as a management tool.) But one thing never survives the process: the stock price. It goes to zero as a company's former equity holders are wiped out and its creditors take control. That means contrarian investors like me don't have to cover our short positions. We make 100 percent on our investment.

Cal Coastal had all the hallmarks of a dead company walking. It was choking on almost $200 million in long-term debt, and its revenues had fallen from a peak of $96 million in 2006 to less than half that in 2007. Meanwhile, sales on its only pending development project—a 110-acre planned community called Brightwater on the Bolsa Chica Mesa near Huntington Beach—were sluggish, to put it mildly. Cal Coastal was planning to put up more than three hundred houses, but so far it had moved a grand total of forty. There was also the minor problem of a Native American burial ground on the property that had sparked some protests and negative media coverage. This was no remake of the movie *Poltergeist.* This was real.

Despite all of its troubles, shorting Cal Coastal was far from a sure thing. The stock was selling near its book value on the morning I flew in to John Wayne Airport. On top of that, almost everyone in the US real estate and financial industries was optimistically predicting that the housing market would rebound following the enormous rise in foreclosures that began in 2006. I was skeptical of this consensus, but I wasn't ready to short Cal Coastal quite yet. A quarter century after my first corporate meeting at Global Marine, I was still following Geoff Raymond's formula: crunch the numbers all you can, but then go see the real people involved before you act. That's why I found myself in Orange County on that beautiful Southern California morning. I was going to give the company's management one last chance to convince me that Cal Coastal wasn't about to collapse.

I pulled my rental car up to a red light and started flipping around the radio for a news station. The light turned green. I lifted my foot off the brake, and just as I started to come down on the gas pedal, an elderly man in a Coupe de Ville slammed into me from behind.

So much for being on time to that meeting.

The accident was no big deal. Nobody was hurt. The cars were barely dented, and the guy in the Cadillac was very apologetic. Once we had exchanged information, I called the rental company, which sent a new car out to me. But the delay had blown my schedule to hell. The Cal Coastal guys were jammed up the rest of the day. I had no other meetings scheduled, and I was due back in the San Francisco Bay Area that evening for dinner. I was torn. Half of me wanted to just head back to the airport and fly standby on the next departure. The other half was telling me to do something completely different—drive out to Bolsa Chica Mesa and take a look at Brightwater for myself.

There's a famous, perhaps apocryphal, story from the late 1920s, of Joseph Kennedy listening in horror as the guy shining his shoes offered him stock picks. According to the story, Kennedy knew right then and there that the market was about to tank. I had a similar moment of clarity looking out at the denuded hills and half-finished homes of the

Brightwater development. The place was an unmitigated disaster. The company was slapping up chintzy McMansions cheek-by-jowl and charging $800,000 for the smallest, cheapest units. I went into one of the few completed model homes and sat down at the mock kitchen table. Through a nearby window, I could see the house next door a few yards away. I imagined some poor homeowner trying to relax in her kitchen while the drone of her neighbor's dishwasher came drifting through the window. As for the development's name, some of the more expensive homes—priced well north of a million dollars—had peekaboo views of the Pacific Ocean off in the distance, but "Brightwater" seemed like a major stretch. *Dimwater* might have been more appropriate, because you had to squint to make it out.

Up to that point, I had had a pretty strong hunch that the housing market wasn't going to recover anytime soon. I'd lived long enough to see real estate implode twice before, first in Houston during the oil bust of the 1980s, then in California in the early 1990s. But it wasn't until I physically set foot on the pale red soil of Bolsa Chica Mesa and saw the debacle-in-progress that I fully understood the magnitude of the downturn we were facing.

I realized something else, too, there on the coast of Orange County: my grandparents probably would have laughed at me for taking so long to figure out how bad things were. People in their generation were very attuned to the pitfalls of the real estate market. They'd lived through the Depression, and because of that they did everything they could to avoid big debts, or at least to minimize their exposure. They used to hold mortgage-burning parties with all of their neighbors when they'd finished paying off their loans. It was a huge relief for them to be clear of the frightening burden of their home loans. I considered how far we'd gotten from that. At the height of the housing bubble, people gladly loaded themselves down with enormous mortgages (and other debts) that they couldn't possibly afford. Then they went on to take out second, third, even fourth mortgages on top of it.

I got on the phone right then with my office and told my trader to short 200,000 shares of Cal Coastal. The company was bankrupt by the end of the following year, and its stock went to zero. I also shorted several other real estate–related companies. But that's not the interesting part of the Brightwater story. I'm not claiming that I was a genius for profiting from the hubris of a badly indebted housing developer hawking vastly overpriced houses on the site of an old Indian burial ground. No. What's interesting is how many people refused to face this reality.

Two weeks before Cal Coastal filed for bankruptcy in October 2009, a well-known analyst at San Francisco–based JMP Securities put out a research report on the company. The stock cost was $1.50 at the time, and the analyst strongly advised his firm's clients to buy it. He predicted that it would hit $5 again in the near future. I couldn't believe what I was reading. Was he talking about the same California Coastal Communities? I had to check twice to make sure.

Fourteen days later, the company officially petitioned for bankruptcy protection. Oops!

Even after Cal Coastal went into Chapter 11, people continued to hope against hope that it would make a comeback. One prominent money manager started to buy Cal Coastal like it was a hot new start-up. There were roughly eleven million common shares of the company. By the time his spree came to an end, this guy had acquired more than two million of them—just in time for the final bankruptcy settlement to wipe out every cent of value they had.

HOW I MAKE MONEY ON FALLING STOCKS

The mechanics of short selling are relatively simple. My prime broker borrows a certain number of shares in a company on my behalf. My fund then sells these borrowed shares at the current market price. Normally, at some point in the future, I would be obligated to purchase that number of shares so that I can "cover" my position.

If the stock in question goes down in value, as I'm expecting, I will be able to buy those shares at a lower price than I sold them for. That's how I make my profit. If the stock goes up, however, covering my position will cost me more than the original price, and I'll have to eat the difference. This is what makes the process more risky than your average investment. Theoretically, there is an infinite amount of risk. If you buy a stock selling at $10, the most you can possibly lose is $10. If you short that same stock, however, and it winds up being the next Apple or Exxon or Berkshire Hathaway, you stand to lose a whole lot more if you don't cover in time.

Ideally, I don't have to worry about covering my positions at all. That's because, unlike most other short-selling investors out there, I don't seek out stocks I think are just going to dip a little bit in the near term (as I did with my very first short of TGI Fridays). I look for genuine failures, companies like Cal Coastal, that seem destined for one outcome: bankruptcy and a zeroed-out stock price.

Neither the analyst nor the fund manager was up to anything under-handed or crooked. They were just catastrophically wrong. And they were far from alone. Almost nobody wanted to face how bad things were in the real estate market. There was a monolithic, if hugely irrational, belief that things would turn around and that prices would start going up again.

I was never heavily invested in real estate stocks. Even at the height of the bubble, I avoided home building and mortgage companies. I knew the real estate market was overheated and that housing had always been a cyclical industry. But even I didn't fully comprehend the enormity of the supercycle disaster we were facing until I set foot on Bolsa Chica Mesa that day and saw all those empty, half-built houses.

In other words, I wasn't like those guys in Michael Lewis's book *The Big Short*. I didn't see the crash coming before the fact. If I had, I'd prob-ably be living on my own private island somewhere. But there's an old saying in the investment game: "It's okay to be wrong; it's not okay to *stay* wrong." As soon as I figured out just how historically massive the downturn was, I adjusted to that reality and began shorting companies in the real estate sector. Pretending that things were going to work out for the best and that the market was going to turn around would have been disastrous. And yet that's exactly what most people did. They stayed in denial right up until they went broke.

Unfortunately, this is how the majority of people in business and investing behave when they're facing hard times and hard choices.

THE LONE STAR STATE OF DENIAL

I got to witness my first full-blown corporate implosion from the inside. Texas Commerce Bank, or TCB as we affectionately called it, started off as an obscure regional bank catering mainly to Houston's wealthy elite. But it grew exponentially during the oil boom of the 1970s. By the time I got there in '83, it was the largest bank in Texas. The Texas Commerce Tower, our headquarters, was the eighth-tallest high-rise on the planet at the time, and everyone who worked there was brimming with enthusiasm.

Then the oil market collapsed, and quite literally overnight, everything changed. I still remember the bleak mood that fell over the staff after our chief financial officer announced that we'd had our first quarterly profit decline in more than sixteen years. The room was tomb silent. No one could believe it. But our CFO, a smart, fast-thinking Harvard- and Stanford-educated Houston native, was quick to reassure us with a clever analogy. "Listen. Everybody remembers when Joe DiMaggio's fifty-six-game hitting streak ended," he said. "But did you know he started another streak the very next day that went on for sixteen more games? We're going to be like DiMaggio, guys. Don't worry. This is just a temporary setback."

He went on to explain why we were going to be like DiMaggio. Unlike most other banks in Texas, he said, TCB hadn't been "lending on iron"—that is, it hadn't allowed energy companies to use their drilling equipment for collateral on loans. He stressed this repeatedly to us. It was very comforting to hear, because after the price of oil cratered, there was a whole lot of idle drilling equipment sitting around reaping nothing but rust. Before the crash, the *Hughes Tool Report* counted almost five thousand land rigs operating in North America. By the time our CFO stood up in that meeting, the number was down to a thousand.

After the meeting, a couple of friends approached me as I was crossing the street to get some coffee. The bank's stock was down six bucks that morning alone. After our CFO's pep talk, they were ready to pool their money and buy a big chunk of shares. I was tempted, but I politely declined. As with Global Marine, I was wary of trying to "catch a falling knife" by calling the bottom of our company's downturn. I was also beginning to suspect that things were considerably worse than anyone was admitting. My boss and I talked regularly with management teams in the energy industry, and a lot of those guys were spouting their own we're-down-but-not-out stories. Nobody offered anything quite as inspired as the tale of Joe DiMaggio's hitting streaks, but they were all equally convinced their firms would bounce back.

My circumspection saved me money. It turned out that Texas Commerce, like just about every other bank in the region, had actually been "lending on iron" in a big way. And like just about every other bank in the region, we went downhill fast because of it. By the end of the 1980s, the ten largest banks in Texas had all either gone under or been gobbled up by larger institutions. Texas Commerce was one of the "lucky" ones that got bought out. Chemical Bank, itself soon to be devoured by Chase Manhattan, took us over shortly before I left. We used to joke ruefully that TCB was now "Chemically dependent."

I'm not saying I foresaw Texas Commerce's demise that morning when my friends tried to get me to go in with them on those shares. But even if I didn't quite realize it at the time, I was learning an important and fascinating lesson about business and human nature: *Failure terrifies people.* They'll do whatever they have to do to downplay it, wish it away, and just plain pretend it doesn't exist. Most of the time, they'll go on living in denial long after the truth of their predicament becomes obvious. Americans are especially prone to this kind of mental contortionism. We have a pathological "can do" faith in our abilities. "Failure is not an option" is one of our favorite sayings. The idea of quitting or giving up is almost *unpatriotic*. This attitude benefits us in many ways as a nation. But when it comes to business, and also investing, this kind of excessive optimism can do more harm than good.

Shortly before our CFO's pep talk, another high-level executive at the bank stopped me in the hall to give me what he considered some critical advice. "A lot of smart kids like you come through the bank, and they use it for a stepping stone," he said. "They stay for a year or two and then they leave. I think that's a huge mistake. Look at me: I've been here forever and I'm happier than anyone I know. This place rewards loyalty, and I'm good at my job because I've got my finger right on the pulse of the company. I know everything that's going on."

A week later, I saw two workmen hauling boxes out of his office. He was a victim of the bank's first-ever round of layoffs. I'm not trying to put this man down for his faith in the bank or make light of his unemployment. I want to use his story to make another point about failure in business. That chat reinforced something else I was beginning to learn: people in management positions, even very senior management positions, are often completely wrong about the fortunes of their own companies. *More important, in making these misjudgments, they almost always err on the side of excessive optimism.* They think their businesses are in much better shape than they actually are. Jerry's rig utilization chart at Global Marine and our own CFO's boasts about Joe DiMaggio only underscored this lesson for me at the time. And, three decades and over 1,400 meetings with other executives later, I can say this tendency is as pronounced as ever.

As I explained in the introduction, the companies I describe in this book failed because their managements committed one or more of six common mistakes. But to a person, those leaders all made an additional error: they allowed their optimism to blind them to the reality of their troubles. We could call this the original sin that led to all of their other miscues. Instead of adjusting their strategies, they chose to believe things would naturally work out for the best and they made up all sorts of comforting rationalizations to prove their rosy predictions.

THE DOCTRINE OF ELITE INFALLIBILITY

One of the primary causes of this unrealistic optimism in the corporate and investing worlds is an almost slavish faith in the capabilities of our country's elite. People seem to think that a degree from a top university inoculates its holder from failure. I can't tell you how many times stock analysts and fellow money managers have tried to convince me that a clearly troubled company would turn around simply because its CEO was a graduate of some distinguished school. "He's a Harvard MBA," they'll say in almost reverential tones, or, "He graduated cum laude from Princeton"—as if those facts alone would be enough to offset overwhelming evidence that, despite their impressive backgrounds, they were running their businesses straight into the ground.

Whenever I hear this special pleading, I think of a guy named Robert Jaedicke. He was an accounting professor at Stanford when I was an undergraduate there. Shortly after I graduated, he became the dean of the business school. He parlayed that prestigious position into a number of lucrative seats on corporate boards, including the chairmanship of the audit committee for Enron. Jaedicke began that job in 1985, around the time I saw Ken Lay speak in the Transco Tower. Jaedicke held the job all the way until the company blew apart in 2001 in the biggest accounting scandal in American corporate history. In retrospect, it's obvious that the only thing the board of Enron managed to audit in all that time were the buffet tables at their meetings. But right up to the end, the impression that such a distinguished figure from a top school like Stanford was overseeing the company's books gave an awful lot of Enron investors a dangerously false sense of security.*

The doctrine of elite infallibility almost cost me a great deal of money, too. In 2007, one of my social friends pitched me on investing some of my own money in a large and exclusive New York hedge fund. He showed me an impressive prospectus and boasted of the fund's steady, double-digit annual returns. I was intrigued but declined his invitation. For one thing, when I asked to have a cup of coffee with the fund's manager the next time I was in New York, my friend said the man never met with potential clients. On top of that, the fund was audited by an obscure accounting firm in New Jersey. That might be all right for a small concern, but this was a multibillion-dollar operation. Finally, the fund's manager didn't keep the performance fee he charged. Instead, he kicked the money back to a worldwide army of asset gatherers, people like my friend, who recruited new investors. All of these facts struck me as more than a little fishy. But after I said no to my friend's offer, I didn't think much about it—until a year later when I turned on the news and saw hedge fund manager Bernard Madoff being perp-walked into a Manhattan courthouse. I dug up the prospectus my friend had given me and discovered that I had narrowly avoided becoming one of the victims of the largest financial fraud in history.

---

*Kathleen Pender, "Ex-Dean of Stanford Business School Led Enron Audit Panel," *San Francisco Chronicle,* February 7, 2002.

When my friend tried to sell me on investing in one of Madoff's "feeder" funds, it took me less than an hour to spot three very troubling issues with his operation. But most people failed to investigate Madoff's business at all before investing. They assumed that someone so prestigious had to be aboveboard. He was friends with senators. He was the former chairman of NASDAQ. The idea that a man of his stature was running a $50 billion Ponzi scheme was unthinkable, so investors gave him fortunes without a second thought. If they'd only taken a few moments to study his business practices, they could have easily identified the same potential problems I saw. These red flags weren't hidden from view. In fact, several years before Madoff's arrest, a whistleblower sent the Securities and Exchange Commission a fifty-page report detailing the obvious fraud. But even the regulatory authorities refused to believe that such a prominent figure was a crook.

It wasn't just elitism that led investors to trust Madoff with their money. Two other factors contributed to their faith. The first was plain old greed. Madoff's phony returns were phenomenal, and phenomenally consistent. Everybody was too busy basking in the money he was supposedly making them to realize that his fund's performance was almost certainly too good to be true. The second factor had to do with identity. For a large number of his investors, Bernie Madoff was "one of us." He was a respected, even revered figure in the Jewish community—and many of his victims came from that world because of it. This is an age-old problem in both business and investing. Call it the country club effect. Even the sharpest, most astute professionals tend to perform less due diligence when they're dealing with someone with whom they have an affinity. Whether these ties are based on ethnic, class, or family background is immaterial. The affinity fallacy happens across all groups.

Fraudsters often play on affinities to avoid scrutiny. Madoff was a master at this. He donated millions to Jewish charities to build up his reputation and strengthen people's trust. Unfortunately, many of those same charities and nonprofits wound up losing huge amounts of money when his scam was uncovered.*

For all the publicity they generate, pure con artists like Madoff are actually quite rare. Most financial and business elites who fail aren't frauds or criminals. Like Robert Jaedicke at Enron, they simply do a poor job. Just about every executive I've ever met boasted impressive, even world-class credentials. You don't get hired for senior management or directorship positions at publicly traded corporations without being well educated, accomplished, and capable. But those positive qualities create negative results when they lead people—and their followers—into overconfidence or hubris. I'm not saying that a successful track record and a degree from a good school are bad things. But they can create a kind of personal historical myopia, a mistaken belief that one's past successes guarantee similar results in the future.

Self-delusion is a powerfully democratic force. It cuts across all social classes. You can be richer, smarter, and more successful than anyone else. But if you're not brutally honest with yourself about your own potential for failure, you're going to have a problem—and you're going to lose money, maybe a lot of money. I should know. Not all my trades have worked out as well as my experience with California Coastal Communities. I've made plenty of losing investments and blown plenty of major opportunities. One of my biggest blunders came only two years after I started my hedge fund. I missed out on a chance to buy in early on a

_____

*Robin Pogrebin, "In Madoff Scandal, Jews Feel an Acute Betrayal," *New York Times*, December 24, 2008.

couple of small but promising companies in the Pacific Northwest. You might have heard of them.

Do the names Costco and Starbucks ring any bells?

WEIGHTED UP

The way stock indexes are calculated feeds investors' excessive optimism by masking how common failure is in the business world. Just about all of them are weighted by market capitalization. That means they're not based purely on the average performance of the companies listed in them. The *size* of those companies is also a major factor. The larger a company's market capitalization, the bigger effect its stock has on the index's value. The S&P 500, the NASDAQ, all the Russell indexes, they're all weighted this way, and most investors have no clue how this distorts their view of the corporate world.

Here's what I mean: a single company with a massive market cap and a rapidly rising stock price often drives an entire index higher even as dozens or hundreds of smaller companies in that same index drop or disappear altogether. From 2005 to 2012, Apple's stock shot up from $40 a share to $700. As it approached its peak, Apple made up more than a fifth of the NASDAQ 100 and almost 12 percent of the entire index. For significant periods of time its growth was responsible for much of the index's gains. That kind of outsized weighting conceals the plain fact that *more stocks in that index went down rather than up over the course of Apple's incredible rally.*

TWO

THE FALLACY OF
FORMULAS

Figures lie and liars figure.

—Anonymous

JERRY, THE GLOBAL MARINE EXECUTIVE, DIDN'T JUST MAKE
the mistake of learning only from the recent past when he told me to buy
the company's stock. He also put way too much faith in his magic rig utilization formula. For Jerry, buying stock in Global Marine at 70 percent
utilization was what they call, in sports betting, a "lock." That's why he
was so relaxed and confident when Geoff Raymond and I met him. But
of course, there's no such thing as a true lock, in sports or in business,
and confusing formulas with good decision making can be disastrous—
not only because formulas can be wrong, but also because if you get too
fixated on a set of numbers or a particular way of doing things, you can
easily miss out on other critical information. I've fallen into that trap repeatedly over the years. But one particular instance still stings, even after
more than two decades.

Blowing a chance to make millions of dollars is hard to forget.

In August 1992, I took a trip up to Seattle to visit the managements of a few up-and-coming companies at the time. My first meeting was with the chief financial officer of Costco (stock symbol: COST), a fellow named Richard. I took a morning flight out of San Francisco and drove across Lake Washington from Sea-Tac airport to the company's corporate headquarters, which were still in Kirkland at the time. On the way, I stopped for my third cup of coffee of the day from, of all places, Starbucks. They'd opened a few stores in the Bay Area by then and I was a fan of their java. OK, *fan* is an understatement. *Hopeless addict* would be a better description.

When Richard came out of his office and extended his hand to me, it took me a minute to realize he was the executive I was scheduled to meet. He looked like he should have been driving a forklift around a Costco warehouse instead of running the company's finances. He was a husky guy with a receding hairline and a dark, bushy mustache. But what really threw me was his outfit. He was wearing baggy blue jeans and a flannel shirt. That was my introduction to the relaxed corporate culture of the Pacific Northwest. A guy dressed like that wouldn't have been allowed in the door of Texas Commerce Bank. But in Seattle, he was the number three man in one of the region's most promising companies.

After recovering from my initial confusion, I shook Richard's hand and he escorted me into his office. That third Starbucks coffee had gotten me pretty revved up. I tend to talk fast anyway, but that morning I was really rolling. Before Richard could say anything, I rattled off all of my reservations about his company. First, I brought up its profit margins. By my calculations, the money Costco cleared on merchandise was so minuscule, most of its profits actually came from the membership dues it charged customers. That led straight into my second issue: What was the deal with charging people to shop in its stores anyway? Was it really a good idea to limit the number of customers it had? Finally, I said I was worried about its biggest competitor at the time, a company called Price Club.

Richard took a moment to make sure I was done and then calmly answered my questions. He may have been dressed like the rhythm guitarist in a grunge band, but he was very, very smart. And to his credit, he didn't try to sell me or spin the truth.

"You're right," he said. "Our margins are quite thin. They're less than 2 percent on most items after overhead. That's why we don't accept credit cards. The banks charge 2 percent for each transaction, so if we took cards, we'd actually be losing money on most sales. That's why we charge a nominal membership fee. It helps ensure that our customers have the means to pay with cash or to write us checks that won't bounce."

"And what about Price Club?" I asked. "How are you going to fend them off?"

"They're a good company, but we're better," he answered confidently. "We're growing faster and we're opening more stores."

I shook Richard's hand again and drove back into Seattle for my next meeting with Orin, the CFO of Starbucks (stock symbol: SBUX). Later on, Starbucks would move into some very plush corporate offices on Utah Avenue. But back then, its executives were still working out of a drab warehouse space near Boeing Field.

Orin was the polar opposite of Richard, at least appearance-wise. He was tall and lean. He wore the typical CFO uniform—khakis and a crisply tucked blue oxford shirt—and the part in his neatly combed blond hair was as straight as a rifle barrel. We had a good chat, very cordial but also to the point. I rarely spend more than an hour in these kinds of meetings. I lay out my concerns and I listen to peoples' answers, then I let them get back to work. That morning, I told Orin I was concerned about spikes in the price of coffee and how those would affect Starbucks' bottom line. Coffee is a volatile commodity. Prices can fluctuate wildly, even in a single trading day. Orin was surprisingly blasé about that fact.

"We've done surveys of our customers as they're leaving our stores," he told me. "We ask them, 'How much did you just pay for that cup of coffee or that latte?' And the majority of them can't remember. They have no idea what they just paid, even though it was only minutes earlier!"

"That's interesting," I said. "But how does that answer my question about coffee prices?"

"What we give people is a little luxury," Orin replied. "They're willing to pay a small premium for it. Big luxuries, like a new car or a new television, those are different. People are very conscious of what they're spending on those kinds of things. But when it comes to our products, they don't care because it's only a couple bucks and it makes them happy. So if the price of coffee beans goes up, we just add a few cents to what we charge. Trust me, nobody notices."

As I drove back to Sea-Tac and considered whether to buy stock in Starbucks and Costco, I thought about the three cups of coffee I'd bought that day—one from a Starbucks location near my house in Mill Valley, one from a kiosk at San Francisco airport, and one on the way to Kirkland. Orin was right. I had absolutely no idea what any of them had cost. I'd plunked down my money and pocketed my change without glancing at it. I was too excited to take that first sip to care whether I'd paid a buck-fifty or two or even three dollars.

The beauty of Starbucks, especially back then, was its consistency. You knew that no matter where you were, the coffee was going taste the same as it did anywhere else, whether it was from a location near the boardwalk in Newport Beach, California, or at the company's original cafe in Seattle's Pike Place Market. That might not sound like much of a big deal now, but this was an extremely novel concept in the early 1990s. Up to that point, it had been hard to find anything better than Folgers in most of America. Sure, there were upscale cafes in cities like Los Angeles, New York, and Seattle, but until Starbucks came around, there was no way to get comparable coffee in most other places.

Costco had a similarly unique business model. It offered cheap prices, just like Kmart, Sears, and the other classic big-box retailers of that era. Unlike those places, however, it sold quality merchandise instead of discount junk. Costco's leaders recognized that people who bought higher-end stuff liked a bargain as much as anyone else. And of course, the company also sold food and beverages—good food and beverages, in bulk, at more or less wholesale rates. It might seem normal nowadays for suburbanites to stock up on cases of fine wine and mayonnaise jars the size of oil drums. But back in 1992, it was downright revolutionary. People went wild for the concept and the company took off. Like Starbucks, Costco was building all over the country, with more stores opening seemingly every day.

There was no doubt in my mind that both of these companies were going to prosper. My gut was telling me to jump in and buy thousands of shares of each. But my head just wouldn't let me. In the end, I talked myself out of investing—and that wound up being an expensive conversation.

In August 1992, a share of Costco was running around $34. Less than a year later, Costco merged with Price Club and its stock split 2–1. It then went on a steady rally until it split again at over $90 per share in 2000. By the beginning of 2014, COST was trading for roughly $120.

Adjusted for splits and dividends, if I'd bought the stock back then and held on to it until 2014, my investment would have gone up over twenty times. But that missed opportunity is actually small compared to my other colossal could-have-been from that trip, Starbucks. If I had bought SBUX after chatting with Orin at the company's old headquarters that morning, it would have been worth over *one hundred times* what I'd put in twenty-two years earlier.

So what went wrong that day in 1992? Why didn't I pull the trigger on the stocks? After all, I thought both companies were winners. I was (and still am) literally addicted to the products one of them offered. And as I found out in person on that trip, they were run by extremely bright, competent managements. So what in the world was my problem?

Put simply, *I was too attached to my formula.* For one, I am very wary of stocks that have recently gone public. I never buy into initial public offerings. Unless you are one of the insiders who gets awarded sharply discounted shares, they are almost always terrible investments. But that wasn't the main reason I shied away from Costco and Starbucks. The biggest rationale was that neither of them added up to a good buy according to my chosen method for picking stocks, something called growth at a reasonable price (GARP) investing.

Back then, there were basically two schools of money management: GARP and value investing. As I discussed in the last chapter, Geoff Raymond was primarily a value investor. He would calculate a company's book value and compare that to its share price to determine if it was undervalued or overvalued. I practiced this method with him at Texas Commerce, but after I left the bank, I came to rely more on GARP to guide me. Despite what happened in Seattle in 1992, I still do.

A GARP investor looks for companies that are growing. Starbucks and Costco certainly were doing that in big ways. But the acronym contains a caveat: at a reasonable price. If a company's earnings are growing fast but its share price is growing faster, the GARP school says to stay away. The way you figure out whether this is the case is by calculating something called the multiple—the ratio of a company's share price to its earnings per share—and comparing it to its rate of growth. When a company's multiple is larger than its rate of growth, the stock is overpriced and thus not a good investment.

At the time of my visit, Costco's stock was actually down from a high of almost $65 a year before. But even at its newly discounted price, by the GARP formula Costco's past and projected earnings were not enough to make the investment worthwhile. Its earnings multiple was quite high, in the thirties. The idea of investing in a company with those kinds of numbers was a big stretch for me, no matter how promising it seemed. Unfortunately, I got the same results when I crunched the numbers on Starbucks. Its price-earnings multiple was also well over thirty. Compared with its recent and projected future earnings, that valuation was simply too high to make it a worthwhile investment. Or so I figured. By which I mean I figured wrong.

One of the main reasons I favor the GARP investing approach is that it helps prevent me from falling prey to manias and groupthink. If a company's stock price is too high compared to its earnings, that generally means one of two things: either its earnings growth has slowed but investors have been reluctant to sell off their holdings, or its stock has been bid up beyond what the company's performance merits. In both of these scenarios, the GARP formula keeps an investor from following the herd. You don't stay invested in overvalued companies, and you don't get caught up in popular, overhyped stocks that are rising too fast.

But here's the catch: sometimes the herd is right.

My rigid adherence to the GARP philosophy kept me from recognizing something important about Starbucks and Costco. There was a good reason their stock prices were so high. They were, and they remain today, *once-in-a-lifetime companies.* Since that visit to Seattle, they have each reinvented their respective industries. They are two of the greatest corporate success stories in the last century. Starbucks in particular has built the greatest American brand since Coca-Cola. Most investors are lucky to get in early on *one* opportunity like that. And I was gift-wrapped the chance to buy into two of them—in one day—and I passed on both.

This is what I mean when I say that fixating on a formula can be disastrous. All real-life rules have exceptions to them. When it came to Costco and Starbucks, I almost recognized this. I strongly suspected that they were both unique companies that defied the usual formulas. But, in the end, I just couldn't pry myself away from my formula, and it cost me an enormous amount of money.

This fallacy happens all the time in management as well as investing. Corporate managers frequently bind themselves tightly to what seems like a winning approach, only to discover after the fact that it was really a noose.

DOUBLE JEOPARDY

One of the first companies I shorted on its way to bankruptcy failed because, just like I did with Starbucks and Costco, the executives in charge wed themselves too strictly to a formula. Soon after my trip to Seattle, I was chatting on the phone with a stock analyst at Chicago-based William Blair, and he mentioned a dollar-store company from Milwaukee called Value Merchants (stock symbol: VLMR). It had started out as a toy retailer, but by the time I learned about it, most of its revenue came from its ubiquitous Everything's a Dollar stores.

"These guys are growing like crazy," the analyst said. "The new CEO has pledged to double the number of locations every single year."

"Double?" I asked incredulously.

"That's right," he replied. "When he took over, they only had sixty Everything's a Dollar stores. They were up to two hundred by the end of the next year. Now, there's over *five* hundred."

"That's insane," I said.

"Maybe, maybe not. But they say they're going to keep it up and double again this year."

I hung up the phone and took a short drive to the nearest Everything's a Dollar outlet in the Northgate Mall in San Rafael, California, a few miles from my office. I'd never been in one of those stores before, and it was a strange experience. The smell of cheap vinyl permeated the place, and the merchandising choices were haphazard, to say the least. Bins of rubber rats and other cheap toys lined the floors beneath plastic sunglasses, costume jewelry, novelty bumper stickers, and shelves of weird generic cereals and toothpaste brands I'd never heard of. After I walked the aisles for a little while, I approached the store manager, a harried-looking woman restocking a table of "I'm with Stupid" T-shirts.

"Excuse me," I said. "How do you decide what items you sell here?"

"I don't decide anything," she answered with a bashful smile. "Every week a truck backs up behind the store, and we offload boxes of merchandise. Then we take all the things that haven't sold in the past week, and we put them in those same boxes and they go back onto the truck."

"Where does that stuff go?"

The woman shrugged, "To the next store, I guess."

Normally, I follow Geoff Raymond's formula for investing: I study a company's fundamentals, and I visit its management before I make a decision on whether or how to invest in it. But I broke that formula in the case of Value Merchants. I didn't bother flying to Milwaukee to meet with its executives. I shorted sixty thousand shares right after I got back to my office. I knew the formula of doubling stores every year was going to be the death of the company. There was simply no way it could manage that kind of hypergrowth.

The company's earnings were already starting to go sour at the time. Even though all those new stores had boosted top-line revenues, profit margins were down. That was hardly surprising. Opening all those stores required major capital outlays. But more important, it kept the company's management from focusing on the most important task retailers—even junk retailers—have to perform: finding things that people actually want to purchase. Just because the stuff on your shelves is cheap doesn't mean consumers will automatically buy it. Even the least-discriminating shoppers out there have to *like* what you're selling.

The store manager's story of weekly deliveries confirmed that the company was headed for disaster. It clearly sourced all of its merchandise from overruns, remainders, or fire sales. There was no way it could return goods that didn't sell to the manufacturers. So where did it all go? Back onto the truck and straight to the next store on its delivery schedule. That next store would then stock this rejected junk and pass its poor-selling

MARATHON MAN

Shortly after my visit to the Everything's a Dollar store in San Rafael, I was chatting on the phone with another stock analyst from Robert Baird, a brokerage that, like Value Merchants, was based in Milwaukee. I happened to mention that I was short Value Merchants. The analyst gasped audibly.

"I know the CEO personally," he said. "He gets up every morning at 4 a.m. He ran a three-hour marathon last year. I'm telling you, he's a competitive beast, Scott. He eats steel for breakfast."

"So what?" I countered.

"So I wouldn't bet against a guy like that."

After I got off the phone, I felt even better about my decision to short VLMR. I was even tempted to increase my position. As I'll discuss later on, people in the investment and business worlds mistakenly overvalue competitiveness. I think it's actually one of the worst qualities you can have, not only because it leads people to put too much faith in their own abilities, but also because it makes them less likely to recognize their mistakes and change course. Competitive types think they can will their way to success, no matter what. But no amount of will can counter a doomed formula—like doubling your number of stores every year.

goods on to the subsequent one and so on and so on. It was a kind of inventory Ponzi scheme. The company was relying solely on new store growth to boost its revenues. But because of that excessive growth, it couldn't possibly bring in enough desirable new merchandise for all those locations, so it was reduced to rotating an increasingly unsellable backlog of crap among its outlets.

Less than twelve months after my trip to Northgate Mall, Value Merchants filed for bankruptcy.

Failed business formulas usually aren't as mathematically precise as Value Merchants' commitment to double in size every twelve months. More generalized "growth for growth's sake" formulas can be just as dangerous, especially when they rely on debt. The airline industry is notorious for debt-fueled expansion, and that's one of the main reasons nearly every major airline has filed for bankruptcy at one time or another.

Another sector that has seen numerous companies fall victim to the growth-is-always-good formula is fast food—known as quick service restaurants, or QSR, in the investment world. Krispy Kreme Doughnuts was a prime example of this fallacy. Instead of granting its new franchisees one outlet at a time and making them prove themselves before allowing them to acquire new locations, as McDonald's does, the company negotiated deals with a handful of "area developers" for exclusive rights to large territories. In exchange, the franchisees guaranteed that they would open at least ten stores in their regions and pay top dollar to the parent company for donut-making equipment and supplies.

On paper, this formula appeared to allow Krispy Kreme to expand quickly across the country. But in actuality it meant that the company had ceded control over the fortunes of its own business. Several of these area developers couldn't live up to the terms of their agreements, and went bankrupt. Normally, the failure of individual franchisees isn't a major blow to a large chain. But because of Krispy Kreme's misguided strategy, customers in many major markets suddenly couldn't find one of its original glazed donuts within five hundred miles.

I experienced this vanishing act firsthand. Whenever we'd visit my parents, I would take my kids out for a late-night treat at a Krispy Kreme store in Chandler, Arizona. One night, much to our dismay, we discovered that it had been shuttered the week before. I drove to a store in Phoenix but it was closed, too, as was every other location in the surrounding area. After a half hour of searching, we broke down and went to Dunkin' Donuts instead.

BY THE BOOK

Over the years, I've seen dozens of companies in all sorts of industries fail because, like Value Merchants and Krispy Kreme, they committed themselves to a formula and stuck with it, even when all the evidence was practically screaming at them to change. I wish I could say my failure to buy into Starbucks and Costco was the only time I committed this mistake myself. But sadly, it wasn't. I once made a major investment in a company that fit all too neatly into my GARP model of stock picking. A few years later, it was bankrupt—because its management, too, refused to rethink a set formula.

For the most part, San Diego–based Advanced Marketing Services (stock symbol: ADMS) did one thing and one thing only: it distributed wholesale books to big-box retailers. Along with Sam's Club, Costco was its main customer. But unlike Costco, Advanced Marketing's price-earnings ratio lagged its earnings growth rate. Its revenues were growing rapidly, thanks mainly to the phenomenal success of Costco, but its share price wasn't rising nearly as fast. According to my GARP formula, that made ADMS a very attractive stock. So after monitoring its performance for a little while, I flew down to Advanced Marketing's headquarters in a business park in northern San Diego.

I love going to San Diego on business. I always wind up my days in Old Town eating Mexican food and drinking margaritas. I sit outside in the sun—by the late afternoon, it is *always* sunny in San Diego—and sip my drink and watch the tourists walk by. Maybe I should blame those margaritas for my not spotting the trouble at Advanced Marketing sooner.

The company's chief financial officer at the time of my first visit was named John. The only way I can think to describe him is *bookish*. He was tall and lanky and very soft-spoken. He could have easily passed for a college professor. At one point he told me that he had originally intended to study for the priesthood before switching to business school. And he seemed to have an almost evangelical faith in the importance of what Advanced Marketing did.

"We give publishers new ways to sell books and we bring more books to consumers," he said.

Even before I flew down to San Diego, I was already almost certain I was going to buy ADMS. I was in love with how neatly its numbers fit into my GARP formula. Buying it also seemed like a cheap way to own Costco without actually paying what still seemed like Costco's inflated share price. But I had one reservation, which I brought up with John: the company was strict about only charging a 15 percent markup on its books, even though it bore all of the expenses for shipping and warehousing them. On top of those overhead liabilities, Advanced Marketing ate the costs of any unsold books its clients dumped back on it.

John granted that the 15 percent rule was risky. "But that's how we stay in the game," he asserted. He went on to describe what should have been an ominously familiar strategy that the company planned to employ to counter its slim margins: "Our competitive markup is what is going to allow us to continue to grow."

"What about returns?" I asked. "Last year, they were close to 25 percent. That's one book coming back for every four that sell."

John said the company was steadily improving those numbers. It had opened its own outlet stores to offload the books that came back. It had also beefed up its advertising and marketing divisions to make sure clients only ordered books that would sell out. To help make this happen, it had started promoting books both inside stores and through media campaigns. The company charged for this service, John added, which gave it an extra revenue stream.

His presentation was quite impressive. And it was hard to argue with the raw numbers. The company was growing like a weed, yet its price multiple was a tempting ten times earnings. After enjoying my customary margarita in Old Town that afternoon, I called my trader and told her to buy 200,000 shares first thing in the morning. For the first few years, ADMS was a GARP gold mine. Just as John had predicted, the company's earnings kept growing. Only now, the share price started to keep pace. Pretty soon, the stock had doubled, and it kept rising. At its peak, it approached $30, almost triple what I had paid only a few years earlier. That's not a bad return on investment—if I had sold in time, that is.

I returned to San Diego a few more times over the next couple of years to meet with Advanced Marketing's management. John left the company and a new CFO named Ed took his place. Ed wasn't much different than his predecessor. He genuinely seemed to love anything and everything that had to do books. The same was true for the founder and chief executive officer. Visiting the company felt more like stepping into a faculty lounge than a corporate office. And every time I came down, executives had nothing but good news for me. Returns were dropping and sales were climbing. The company was even buying up competitors and other players in the book distribution game.

If I'd been paying more attention, though, I would have noticed that something was definitely amiss. For a company that specialized in books, its own financial books were as hard to figure out as a good Agatha Christie whodunit. As Ed was fond of pointing out for me, the company's sales kept growing every year. Yet its profit margins were actually heading south. For the last fiscal year I owned the stock, 2003, the company's net sales were up 21 percent from the year before, but its net income was cut in half. You don't need an MBA to know that rising revenues and falling profits do not reflect a sterling business model.

Company management kept putting out press releases claiming that the company was on the verge of solving the issue. They were improving their inventory software, they were cutting overhead, they were streamlining their distribution centers. But none of these measures brought margins back up. It was like bailing out the *Titanic* with a tennis racket. They were working furiously but the ship kept taking on water.

Around this time, I was at the American Electronics Association Conference in Monterey, California, and I ran into a guy I went to business school with who was (and still is) one of the greatest investors in the country. He managed his fund at Fidelity from a couple hundred million dollars to something like $35 *billion*. I'm going to spend a fair amount of time in this book bad-mouthing money managers—and the vast majority of them deserve it—but this guy is an exception. When I saw him at the AEA, I realized that he had the same last name as the CEO of Advanced Marketing, so I asked him if they were related.

"He's my cousin," the man replied.

"That's great," I said. "You know, I own the stock."

He gave me a look like a bad smell had just wafted into the conference room.

"I wouldn't go near that company," he said. "Their margins are too small. It's a terrible business."

I walked away wondering if I should dump my stake. But even after hearing that a money manager as successful as my old classmate wasn't willing to invest in his own cousin's company, I just couldn't let go.

Just one year after Advanced Marketing's stock hit its apex, the company struck an iceberg. By the time I recognized what was happening and sold my holdings, its share price was below what I had paid. Worst of all, I didn't see it coming. I was too busy being proud of myself, and my formula, to notice that the company was foundering. I allowed myself to trust management's assurances instead of studying the numbers closely myself. In other words, I believed what I wanted to believe—that my GARP formula had delivered a winner. The illusion worked for a little while. But blissful ignorance has a short shelf life.

As it turned out, things were worse at Advanced Marketing than anyone knew. It wasn't just another troubled company with low margins. It was a fraud, a miniaturized version of bigger and more famous phonies like Enron or Tyco or WorldCom. A year after I finally sold my shares, the FBI raided the company's offices. A couple of lower-level executives eventually pled guilty to inflating the firm's numbers by about 20 percent. I was stunned when I found this out. I just couldn't imagine guys like John or Ed being involved in something like that. And it's important to note that none of the company's top managers were ever implicated.*

Advanced Marketing is a classic example of how hard it is to spot frauds. As is often the case, the fraud at the company was perpetrated by a handful of employees in a single department. They were doctoring their accounting statements and charging for promotional activities that they never performed. There was simply no way an outside investor like me could have detected these activities. What I could have—and should have—noticed was something much more prosaic: Advanced Marketing's margins were simply too small for the company to survive.

Some fund managers specialize in ferreting out and shorting the stocks of so-called promotes, businesses that put out bogus earnings statements to boost their stock price. But exposing crooked corporations is time-consuming, arduous, and risky work. Not only that, as I said in the introduction, frauds are exceedingly rare. Despite the amount of press they get, there just aren't that many of them out there. The overwhelming majority of companies that go under every year are garden-variety failures. To this day, I still believe Advanced Marketing fit better into this far more common category. It was well on its way to failure before the FBI raided its offices. Accounting tricks didn't kill it; clinging to a flawed formula did.

THE BIRTH OF A CONTRARIAN INVESTOR

Amazingly, even with its lousy business model and investigations into its accounting practices, Advanced Marketing limped along for quite a

---

*Penni Crabtree, "Feds Accuse Ex-AMS Exec of Fraud Role," *San Diego Union Tribune,* March 3, 2005.

while. It didn't declare bankruptcy for another four years after I unloaded my position. Though it seems surprising, this kind of longevity is actually quite common. A lot of companies that have no business staying in business manage to hang on way longer than they should. I first spotted this tendency early in my career when I was managing mutual funds for a company called GT Capital in San Francisco. My focus was investing in smaller, lesser-known companies, and I couldn't help but notice that a lot more stocks in that sector went down sharply than doubled or tripled in price. I also detected another intriguing trend. While many stocks declined in value, they would frequently not go down *enough*. Even the stocks of the most severely troubled businesses would often continue trading at much higher prices than they should have, and for far longer than they had any right to. Time after time, I would study a company's financial statements and be mystified that its share price was anywhere over a penny. And yet people would still be buying the stock.

Even after all these years, I still don't know exactly why this happens, but I think it's due to the same excessively positive outlook I witnessed among the executives at Texas Commerce after the oil bust. Americans' can-do optimism extends to their investing habits, especially when it comes to smaller companies. They like to think that the little guy will prevail, that the plucky entrepreneur with the novel new product or service will catch fire. And of course, company managements are all too happy to encourage this false hope. Like Advanced Marketing's brass, they constantly churn out upbeat press releases about better days to come. Meanwhile, their revenues keep falling, their debt loads keep rising, and their creditors keep circling closer and closer.

While I was at GT, I was forced to watch this potentially lucrative dynamic from the sidelines. As a mutual fund manager, I was not permitted to short stocks. Again and again, I would spot companies that were heading down the drain, with stock prices far above where they should have been, but there was no way to take advantage of those opportunities. It was frustrating. On top of that, I was getting my first lesson in just how corrupt the mutual fund industry is. After I started having success, GT began to market my funds quite literally to death, sucking in more and more assets even though I kept warning the company that doing so would kill the returns I might earn. Meanwhile, the head of US operations got caught using his expense account for things like tennis lessons for his kids and rent payments on his girlfriend's luxury apartment. Shortly after the company fired him, GT was sold to the Bank of Liechtenstein—just in time for that bank's European CEO to be indicted in a massive insider trading scheme.

Thankfully, a friend and mentor of mine named Gary Smith gave me a chance to escape GT. He offered to set me up with my own hedge fund in exchange for a fifth of my profits over five years. I'll talk more about Gary later, but for now I'll just say that I didn't have to think too hard about accepting his terms. By that point, I was sick of the mutual fund racket. But the main reason I said yes was because I was pretty sure I could reap big returns by shorting the stocks of troubled companies.

I started my hedge fund on December 1, 1990, with roughly $3 million under management, including $80,000 of my own money and $300,000 from my brother and my parents. A decade later, it was approaching $200 million. At that point, I stopped accepting new investors because, given the limited liquidity of small cap stocks, my fund was getting too large for my strategy to remain effective. I am not a "permabear" like some of my short-selling friends. I don't believe the markets are always destined to fall. Most of the time, I have more money invested

AN INAUSPICIOUS BEGINNING

One of my former bosses at Texas Commerce hired me on at GT Capital and put me in charge of about $60 million. That's not chump change, but compared to a lot of mutual funds, it was pretty modest. That suited me just fine. I planned to outperform other funds by researching and investing in smaller companies. What's the old saying? If you want to make the devil laugh, tell him your plans? Less than a month after I started at GT, I came into work on the morning of October 19, 1987. You might know that particular date by its more famous name: Black Monday. I grabbed a cup of coffee, sat down at my desk and watched in horror as just about every stock I had inherited hemorrhaged value. By the end of the day, the funds I managed were down 40 percent. Before I was even able to start implementing my new approach, I was already deep in the hole.

GT Capital laid off a third of its US workforce in the next few weeks. To this day, I still don't know why I wasn't fired. But for some reason they kept me on and I kept to my plans. I sought out small, fast-growing companies to invest in, and long story short, things went quite well. Despite our losses on Black Monday and the frustrating fact that I couldn't take advantage of all the short opportunities I saw, by the end of the next year, my funds had all beaten the S&P 500 Index by between 15 and 20 percent. Lipper Analytical Services rated one of them the Number One Growth Fund in America. I was thirty years old and making $80,000 a year. I was recently married. My wife and I were living on Nob Hill in San Francisco and expecting our first child. Aside from the political turmoil inside GT, life was pretty good.

long than I do short. But I would never have been as successful as I have been without the freedom and the flexibility to short stocks.

LET YOUR FINGERS DO THE WALKING

Let's move forward in time again to late 2008. Shortly after my trip to Southern California to discover the doomed Brightwater development on Bolsa Chica Mesa, I flew to Dallas to interview the chief executive officer of a company that still produced the Yellow Pages. For you kids out there, the Yellow Pages was a big yellow book that used to be in every house in America. Before the days of Google and smartphones, if you wanted to find the phone number for a plumber, a pizza place, a stained glass manufacturer, or anything else, you had to haul this giant tome out of a drawer and physically leaf through the pages until you found the listing. As their slogan said, you "let your fingers do the walking."

Believe it or not, this company—known at the time as Idearc (stock symbol: IAR)—was not the only remaining publicly traded Yellow Pages company left in existence. There were two. The other one was in Chicago. Not only that, if you looked at a certain set of numbers, Idearc seemed like a good investment. That might sound outrageous, but it's true. Despite the fact that it produced a hopelessly obsolete product, according to a popular value investing formula, Idearc was a solid buy.

A lot of investors rely on a calculation known as EBITDA to evaluate companies. Like GARP, it's an acronym. It stands for earnings before interest, tax, depreciation, and amortization. People compare a company's EBITDA numbers to its stock price as an alternative to price-to-earnings figures or in conjunction with them. I won't go into the nitty-gritty details of it all, but suffice to say, when you plugged Idearc's numbers into the EBITDA equation, this stagnant company printing an antiquated and soon-to-be-extinct directory came out smelling like a rose. How is that possible? The magic of formulas. As you can imagine, Idearc had shrinking revenues and it was loaded down with debt, too. But it was being run by a smart, savvy former venture capitalist, and he was cutting costs aggressively enough to keep the company's EBITDA looking respectable.

He was also a brilliant salesman. That day in Dallas, he pitched me hard to invest in the company. Idearc's offices were in the old Braniff Airlines headquarters, next to the runways at Dallas–Fort Worth airport. His office had huge floor-to-ceiling windows. As he tried to convince me to buy the company's stock, jumbo jets took off and landed behind him. I'll describe this meeting in more detail later on, but for now I'll just say the CEO's efforts were in vain. There was no way I was going to invest in a massively indebted, money-losing company that made an obsolete product, no matter how good its financial numbers looked when you plugged them into a certain formula. But Idearc's EBITDA figures did convince me *not* to short it. That was a big mistake. The company went bankrupt shortly after that trip to Dallas. I was furious with myself. Once again, I'd gone against my better instincts and allowed a formula to cost me the chance to make a good chunk of money. But luckily for me, the story didn't end there.

Like a zombie in an old monster movie, Idearc emerged from bankruptcy and came back from the dead in early 2010 as a newly reorganized company called Supermedia (stock symbol: SPMD). Thanks to people's blind faith in formulas, SPMD was actually one of the hottest stocks on Wall Street for a brief period of time. You read that correctly. In 2010, a company that derived almost all of its revenues from Yellow

Pages—*Yellow Pages!*—was one of the hottest stocks on Wall Street. I've still got a list of the firms that owned big interests in Supermedia. It reads like a who's who of the investment game: Goldman Sachs, Merrill Lynch, RBS, J.P. Morgan, Fidelity, GE, Babson, Vanguard—they all owned it. Why? Because if you just looked at the numbers and ignored the minor fact that the company produced a completely outmoded product, then Supermedia was a winner.

If you don't believe me, consider this. I still have a copy of a research report the brokerage Oppenheimer & Co. put out in which it rated SPMD an "outperform" stock, boasting that the company "trades at 5x/6x our 2010/2011 EBITDA estimates."* There it is. The culprit, the root of Supermedia's irrationally exuberant rally: the EBITDA formula. The report is dated March 17, 2010. On that date, less than a year after its former incarnation, Idearc, bit the dust, a share of SPMD was $39.65— and Oppenheimer predicted it would hit $50. The stock never made that target. Just prior to the report, it had come close. It went north of $45 a share at one point. But a company can only defy the laws of financial gravity for so long, no matter how many Wall Street brokers want to believe otherwise.

Supermedia was a troubled company with an obsolete product, falling revenues, and ocean-sized debt obligations. In other words, in money manager David Rocker's formulation, it wasn't a fraud, it wasn't a fad, it was just a good old-fashioned failure. And thanks to Wall Street's misguided enthusiasm for it, it was also a goldmine opportunity. I'd missed my chance with Idearc a year earlier. I wasn't going to blow it again.

---

*Ian A. Zaffino and Brian J. Bittner, "SuperMedia Inc. Attractive Near-Term Opportunity, Despite Undeniable Secular Headwinds," Oppenheimer & Co., March 17, 2010.

Now, I should say that even though I was sure—about as sure as one can be about anything in investing—that Oppenheimer's rosy predictions were wrong, I did not rush to short Supermedia when it was near its peak. I waited until it was all the way down to $10 before I pulled the trigger. You might wonder about that strategy. Didn't that leave a bunch of profit on the table? Sure. But by waiting, I saved myself a lot of risk, too. Generally, I hold off until a failing company's stock has lost at least half the value of its 52-week high before I initiate a short. I want it to have enough downward velocity that there's little chance it will stop before it hits bottom. When a stock is up near its peak for the year, like SPMD was when Oppenheimer put out its report, every trader from Frankfurt to Manhattan to Tokyo is going to tune in, and a lot of them are going to wind up buying it, no matter how bad the underlying fundamentals are. If you short the stock at that point, you might make more money, but you also might have to sweat for weeks, months, or even years while the thing continues to rally. And you might just lose a bundle in the end.

Investors perform in irrational ways sometimes, and even junk stocks can live on well past their expiration dates. Advanced Marketing stayed in business for a full five years after I sold my shares. Its stock even went on a couple of sustained rallies, despite the fact that the company was being investigated by the Securities and Exchange Commission and the FBI. If I had shorted ADMS in 2002, I would have been sitting around sweating for half a decade before I made any money. Even Supermedia managed to stave off complete annihilation. In early 2013, it went through bankruptcy and merged with the only other publicly traded Yellow Pages company left standing and became Dex Media (stock symbol: DXM). By the middle of that year, believe it or not, the stock of this new incarnation of Supermedia and Idearc was actually north of $20 again.

Despite its problems, there were still plenty of people out there willing to believe it would recover.

I'm not immune to this tendency to hold on to troubled ventures. I'm pretty good at cutting my losses when it comes to stocks I own. But I'm not just a fund manager. I'm also a budding restaurateur. So far, I've owned two eateries. The second one is still open and it's doing great. The first one was a much different story, however. It failed miserably. Looking back, it was doomed from the start. Yet I kept throwing money at it until the day it quite literally washed out. That's right—I've personally owned a dead company walking, and it wasn't pretty.

SQUEEZED

Sometimes it's not irrationality that keeps the stocks of troubled companies afloat, it's raw aggression.

So-called momentum investors will seek out stocks at or near their 52-week highs that also have a good number of short investors. They'll bid the price up even more, hoping to scare short-sellers into exiting their positions en masse, which serves to inflate the stock even further. It's called a short squeeze, and it's a brutal thing to live through when you're on the receiving end. By waiting until a stock has already shed more than half its peak value, I may sacrifice some potential gains, but I make more over the long run by avoiding these sorts of risks.

THREE

A MINOR OVERSIGHT

Your Customers

Success is a lousy teacher. It seduces smart people into thinking they can't lose.

—Bill Gates

Treat your customers like they own you, because they do.

—Mark Cuban

ONE HOT, STICKY AUGUST EVENING DURING MY FIRST SUM-mer in Houston, my friend Bob Gaughan took me to a restaurant called the Atchafalaya River Cafe out on Westheimer Road. We sat down at a table outside, and he ordered me a bowl of something I had never heard of—gumbo.

I don't think I would be exaggerating if I said that my first taste of gumbo changed my life. It was a revelation to me. The spices, the complex flavors of the roux mixing with the Andouille sausage and the okra and the shrimp, it all went off like a gunshot on my palate. I absolutely loved it. I could have sat there sweating in the humid Houston air all night long with Bob, drinking beer and eating that amazing food. And that's exactly what we did. We went down the menu and I tried just about everything they had. I was so full by the time we left, I could barely walk to the car.

After I started making a little bit of money as a money manager, I went out to eat as often as I could. It was my way of decompressing. And Cajun food was my favorite cuisine. I went back to the Atchafalaya River Cafe regularly. There were plenty of other places to go in Houston. I also made the trip to New Orleans a number of times and tried all the famous spots there: K-Paul's, Commander's Palace, Antoine's. But I have to say, overall, Houston probably has better Cajun food than New Orleans. It doesn't get nearly as much press for it. But the food there is more authentic.

Then I moved back to the Bay Area to manage mutual funds for GT Capital. As far as Cajun food went, it was like moving to the moon. At the time, you couldn't find a good bowl of gumbo within a thousand miles—and believe me, I tried. There was exactly one restaurant in the whole city of San Francisco that served it, a place on Fillmore Street called the Elite Cafe. It's still there. The food wasn't all that bad. It just wasn't up to the standards I was used to. You have to understand, I was a fiend for that food. I craved it. And even though the rest of my life was going great, I was constantly wishing that I could jet back to the South for dinner.

Eventually, I decided to bring the South to me. That's right—I used some of the money I was making by scouting out dead companies walking to go into one of the most failure-prone sectors in the business world—the restaurant game. Ironically (or maybe fittingly), my first attempt at being a restaurateur went down in flames. But that's not the interesting part. Restaurants, especially first restaurants, fail all the time. What's interesting about my experience is how blind I was to a very common mistake that I was making. As an investment manager, I've shorted dozens of businesses in all sorts of other sectors because they've made the exact same error. And yet, as often happens with business leaders, I was so caught up in my own passion and the work of bringing it to life, I couldn't see that, just like those other failed companies, I had neglected to account for a relatively important factor in the success of any venture.

My customers.

I could write a whole book on the misadventures of that first restaurant. It would definitely be a comedy, even though it might make me cry to relive it all. Like how I signed the lease on a location in downtown Mill Valley, California, exactly one week after the 9/11 attacks (not exactly a propitious time to open an eatery). Or how I guaranteed a credit card for my first chef and wound up on the hook for $10,000 for what I later learned were hair plugs (even though, as far as I could remember, he had a healthy mane of hair!). Then there was the time another of the five different chefs I went through decided to get into a good old-fashioned fistfight with one of the five different general managers I hired and fired in the place's three years of existence. Thankfully, the altercation took place after closing, but it didn't do much for the staff's already low morale or mine. Neither did the time the overnight cleaning crew set off the building's sprinkler system. After being called by the fire department at 3 a.m., I watched the sun come up while standing in ankle-deep water in the middle of our dining room.

Of course, every restaurant has troubles. But if you're losing between ten and twenty thousand dollars a month of your own money, like I was, those troubles are a lot harder to put up with. I was shelling out the equivalent of an all-expenses-paid vacation to Cancun every week to lose sleep and babysit my dysfunctional kitchen team, not to mention the twenty-something GM I fired after he put a dish on the menu called "Airline Chicken" without consulting me. As he argued, that was the *technical* term for the cut of chicken purchased from our supplier. But would you order something called "Airline Chicken"? I didn't think so. Neither did anyone else.

The thing that hurt the most, though, and kept me believing that we could turn things around, was that the food itself was out of sight. The CEO of Il Fornaio, Mike Hislop—one of the finest restaurant operators in the Bay Area—told me that he had one of the best meals of his life at my restaurant. He said the flavors were "explosive." That was my opinion, too, and by that point I'd spent almost twenty years trying every Cajun food place I could find. And yet, as good as the menu was, I might as well have been serving blackened hundred-dollar bills for all the money I was losing. And you know what? It was my own fault. In the end, it wasn't goofballs like my pugnacious chef or the "Airline Chicken" GM who caused the place to fail. It was me. I was making a classic mistake. I was mixing up what I liked with what my customers wanted.

Let me say up front that Marin County is gorgeous. The weather is great, the scenery is breathtaking, the air is ocean fresh. I can drive ten minutes and be on top of a mountain overlooking the rugged Pacific Coast. Another ten minutes and I'm at the beach. If I go fifteen miles in the other direction, I'm in San Francisco, one of the best cities in the world. But let's be frank: Marin County is not terribly exciting. Most of the people are old and getting older. Sure, a lot of them used to be hippies and flower children. Some of them did amazing, even revolutionary things several decades ago. But when you get down to it, they're really not that much different than elderly people everywhere. They might drive Priuses with "Free Tibet" bumper stickers instead of Buicks with NRA decals, but they're just as stuck in their ways as your average retiree in Florida and Arizona.

Put simply, opening a place in Mill Valley that specialized in white southern cuisine was like opening a California cuisine restaurant deep in the bayous of Louisiana. It was just a bad fit. Most people in town half-expected me to hang a Confederate flag in the window. That was pretty much what the food represented to them: southern, fried, and fattening. In other words, the exact opposite of what most Marin County diners want to spend their money on. But because I loved the food so much, and because I knew that all of those preconceptions about it are wrong, I believed I could change their minds and bring them over to my opinion. Over a million dollars later, I finally got the message: they weren't going to change.

After my place closed, the next tenant opened a restaurant with a fairly generic menu—salmon, steak, garlic mashed potatoes, salads, some pasta dishes. Even though there are probably three dozen places serving almost identical fare in the vicinity, their dining room is jammed every night. Meanwhile, two years after I gave up on bringing southern food to Mill Valley, I opened another Cajun place across the bay in Berkeley, a college town with a younger, more diverse, and food-savvy population. On average, I'd say the food is no better than my first restaurant's. But this new business is booming. We just leased the space next door and doubled our square footage to accommodate the crowds.

There's no doubt in my mind that my first restaurant was doomed from the start by my own stubborn belief that I could convince people in

Marin to love Cajun cuisine as much as I do. That stubbornness cost me a lot of money. In my experience, I actually got away fairly cheaply, though. I've seen lots of other people and companies lose a hell of a lot more trying to market something their target customers wanted nothing to do with.

The business media loves to laud idiosyncratic visionaries who disrupt their industries by introducing unconventional new products or services. Steve Jobs famously eschewed market research and claimed that he and his team built the first Mac computers for themselves, not their customers. Jobs was also famous for bragging that consumers didn't know what they wanted until he showed it to them. This self-centered approach worked out for him and a few other uniquely gifted innovators. But for every Steve Jobs, there are countless corporate leaders who have lost everything trying to remake their customers' habits.

In 2012, JCPenney's (stock symbol: JCP) management team famously "fired its customers" by eliminating coupons and stocking more expensive brand-name merchandise. The problem was that the people who shopped at JCPenney *liked* using coupons. They enjoyed the feeling that they had discovered bargains, even on no-name or knockoff brands. For many of them, that experience was the main reason they went to JCPenney in the first place, and they stopped coming to the stores after it was taken away from them. These disastrous changes wound up losing the company more than a billion dollars in a single year. They also got the CEO who instituted them, Ron Johnson, unceremoniously canned after only eighteen months on the job. I'll talk about Johnson's absentee management style later on, but his doomed upscale strategy shows the dangers of confusing your own tastes with the tastes of your customers. Shortly after Johnson's ouster, I visited the retailer's offices in Plano, Texas. A longtime executive there gave a simple reason for his former

CEO's failure: "He wanted to make JCPenney into a place where he and his friends would shop."

Johnson had previously overseen Apple's retail stores, and just like I did with Cajun food in Marin County, he tried to foist his personal preference for luxury retail onto the people who patronized JCPenney. According to the executive I met with, not only did Johnson get rid of coupons and bring in more upscale brands, he also curtailed advertising in Spanish and reduced the company's "Big and Tall" inventory, which had once accounted for a significant portion of JCPenney's revenue. These actions practically hung a sign on the front of every JCPenney with Ron Johnson's face on it and the caption, "If you aren't a fit, affluent yuppie like me, don't bother coming in here. We don't want your money."

Of course, there are plenty of profitable businesses that cater primarily to higher-earning customers. Johnson's old employer Apple is a prime example. But JCPenney was never going to transform itself into a luxury brand like Apple or Saks or Lexus. Most of its thousand-plus locations are in middle- and working-class areas, and nearly one hundred of them are in its home state of Texas. You know who lives in Texas in huge numbers? *People who speak Spanish!* You know who else? People who could use a little extra room in the waistline of their pants. Both of these groups had been loyal JCPenney patrons. If Johnson had gotten past his own class biases, he would have recognized that both groups represented major future opportunities for the company too. Any demographer will tell you that Spanish speakers are one of the fastest-growing populations in the country, and lord knows Americans aren't getting any skinnier. Yet Johnson was so eager to remake JCPenney in his own image, he purposely alienated these fast-growing customer bases, perhaps permanently.

Incredibly, getting rid of coupons, stocking prohibitively expensive brands, and turning off Hispanic and big and tall patrons might not have been the worst ways Johnson "fired" JCPenney's core customers. He also removed most of the cash registers in the company's stores and gave sales-people handheld iPads to conduct credit card–only transactions instead. Shoppers who wanted to use cash for their purchases had to schlep their items to special areas, often in remote parts of the stores. That's right— JCPenney made cash-paying customers *work* to spend their money. And since a good number of those customers were "unbanked," without tradi-tional bank accounts or credit cards, this disastrous strategy only made them feel even more unwelcome. The executive I met with estimated that roughly a quarter of all transactions at JCPenney's checkouts were in cash. Take a wild guess how much same-store sales dropped in Johnson's first and only full year as CEO. That's right—25 percent, or $4 billion.*

Not to pile on, but I can't help but share one more of Johnson's fol-lies. The executive I spoke with also told me that Johnson personally disliked the look of antitheft sensors. He thought they made the clothing on sale look cheap—his kind of people would never shop in stores with ugly plastic sensors clipped to the merchandise!—so he ordered them removed. "Our 'shrink' doubled overnight," the executive recounted with a sigh, using the retail industry term for the amount of items stolen or misplaced.

Ron Johnson might go down in history as the poster child of alien-ating a business's core customers, but he was far from the first CEO to make this mistake. In the 1980s, Cadillac did the same thing as JCPen-ney, but in reverse. Instead of trying to sell upscale items to downscale

---

*Matt Brownell, "JC Penney CEO Ron Johnson Out," *DailyFinance*, April 8, 2013.

buyers, Cadillac tried to market cheaper, more compact models like the Cimarron. But no one buys a Cadillac to demonstrate thrift or to save money on gas. People buy Cadillacs to show the world that they can afford to buy a Cadillac. They want them big, powerful, and as ostentatious as possible. They sure as hell don't want something that looks like a glorified Chevy. This misreading of its customers almost brought the venerable brand to ruin. It took Cadillac decades to recover.

Of course, established companies shift strategies all the time. Many succeed in doing so. But just as many, if not more, forget the basic buying habits of their customers in the process. Sometimes managements get so emotionally attached to their creations, or so convinced that they've discovered a unique market need, that they wind up being the last people on Earth to realize that nobody else shares their opinion. Investors are also susceptible to this overconfidence. They buy into a company that they themselves patronize, or that they are convinced creates an indispensable product or service, and they often ignore very compelling evidence that the rest of the market does not share their tastes. It's called confirmation bias—believing what you want to believe and discounting contrary information—and it has destroyed countless portfolios and businesses alike.

FAD ON WHEELS

You may remember that, for a little while, inline skates, known popularly as Rollerblades, were the must-have sporting goods item in this country. My son wanted some so badly, I couldn't even get him to wait for Christmas to get them. He was about ten at the time, and every time he turned on the TV, he saw ads with ecstatic kids flying down the street. It drove him crazy. Finally, I broke down and took him to the store to get a pair.

The first letdown happened right after he took his new toys out of the box. They had so many straps and laces and hooks, it took the two of us fifteen minutes to get them on his feet. It was like donning moon boots or gearing up for a scuba dive. After we finally managed to get him in the things, he took off down the driveway, fell on his rear end, and promptly decided he wasn't so thrilled with inline skates after all. He never wore them again.

Around that time, I was at a Hambrecht & Quist conference in San Francisco, and I saw the two guys running First Team Sports Inc. (stock symbol: FTSP), one of the biggest makers of inline skates, give a presentation. Their stock, like their product, was a hot item at the time. Now, most corporate presentations at stock conferences are absurdly optimistic, but this speech was downright silly. They had charts with sales projections literally turning vertical and flying up off the top of the page. I didn't stay for the whole thing. But I did call an analyst handling the stock at Hambrecht & Quist a couple days later.

"Is this Rollerblade thing for real or is it going to go the way of the Slinky and the Hula Hoop?" I asked her.

"Oh, no," she answered breathlessly. "Rollerblades are here to stay. They're huge and they're only going to get more popular as time goes on."

After I expressed skepticism about this claim, she came back with the most preposterous prediction I have heard in thirty years of listening to preposterously optimistic predictions from analysts, executives, and entrepreneurs: "Mark my words, Scott," she pronounced. "In ten years' time, for every one bike you see in Golden Gate Park on a sunny day, you're going to see ten people on Rollerblades."

"Let me ask you a question," I said. "Do *you* Rollerblade?"

"Absolutely!" she exclaimed. "So do all my friends. I do it every morning before work. It's the best workout you can get!"

I thanked her for her time, hung up the phone, and promptly shorted the stock of First Team Sports. At the time, it was around $6, and to hear people in the business talk, it was quickly heading higher. But when sales stopped growing, the stock made a sharp U-turn. I didn't wait for it to go all the way to zero. I covered my position when it hit $2, shortly before the company was bought out with its stock still clinging to life at $1 a share.

Betting against First Team Sports was not a sure thing. Shorting a company selling a fad product is a very tricky game. Even if you're convinced that their popularity isn't going to last, you still can't tell when it's going to fade. It could take years. But my conversation with the Hambrecht & Quist analyst convinced me that inline skates were going to wipe out sooner than later.

The average Wall Street analyst or institutional salesperson is three things: young, affluent, and hypercompetitive. In other words, people like that analyst I spoke with are the prime demographic for a fad fitness product like inline skates. But most Americans are not like your average person on Wall Street. Sure, for a couple years, the skates sold well, mainly because everybody's kids harangued them into buying a pair. But I was pretty sure most of those buyers had the same letdown as my son did once they actually tried the things. They were simply too awkward to wear and too difficult to master.

First Team's stock was trading at thirty times the company's earnings when I shorted it. That big of a multiple is a major red flag. But the Hambrecht & Quist analyst and the rest of her Rollerblading friends in the industry failed to recognize that clear danger sign. All they knew was that *they* loved inline skating and so did everyone in their social circle, and they made the crucial error of assuming that the rest of the country would follow their lead.

In my opinion, the ultracompetitiveness that makes many money managers fall for fad fitness gear is a terrible trait for any investor. Yet

OFF TRACK

Inline skates were far from the first exercise product to get over-hyped in the money management world. There have been many of them over the years. Remember NordicTrack? It was a big, heavy, expensive contraption built to simulate the workout you got from cross-country skiing. In the late 1980s, two Harvard MBAs bought out the little mom-and-pop company in Minnesota that had invented it. They both loved the thing, and just like that analyst I spoke with about Rollerblades, they assumed that average Americans would, too.

NordicTrack was especially popular in the investment community. No surprise there. Like I said, the industry is full of young, rich strivers with plenty of money to burn on the latest gear for self-improvement. But, as it turned out, most consumers weren't interested in paying hundreds of dollars for something that would take up half their living room and looked like a prop from the movie *Robocop*. It took a few years, but NordicTrack, like inline skates, went off the rails. Its parent company, CML Group, declared bankruptcy in 1998.

most brokerage firms actively seek out competitive people to work for them. Montgomery Securities in San Francisco used to recruit, almost exclusively, former college athletes. They liked the fire and the discipline that the ex-jocks brought to the job. To be sure, those are good attributes for salespeople. But the real reason Montgomery coveted jocks was for their competitiveness, their obsession with winning at all costs. And that, in my opinion, is a very destructive quality. It's actually the last thing you should want in someone handling your money. Why? Because *quitting is very important when you're buying and selling stocks.*

I'm not perfect at what I do, by any stretch, but I am a very good quitter. I'd say I'm one of the better quitters I know. And that skill has helped me a lot over the years.

Take my experience with Advanced Marketing in chapter 2. I blew my chance to profit on that stock when it was still trading at its peak. And I was so enamored with my GARP formula that I exacerbated my mistake by waiting too long to get out. But as soon as I recognized my misreading of the company, I sold right away. I didn't even wait to find out why the stock was going down. I just pulled the rip cord and parachuted out. And while I wound up losing all of the profits I would have made if I'd been more perceptive and sold earlier, I didn't make excuses and hold on as the stock crashed. That's usually the way it goes for me. I might sacrifice some profits, or miss out on chances to make more, but aside from running restaurants in Marin County, I rarely give up large sums of money. And there's one reason for that: I'm a great quitter—and proud of it.

The fact that more companies fail than succeed means, as an investor, you're going to have to deal with losing investments. Excessively competitive people have a hard time accepting this reality. They overestimate their own abilities and their own chances of success. Worst of all, they are reluctant to give up when things turn bad. That's the real danger of competitiveness. Remember the old saying: "It's okay to be wrong; it's not okay to *stay* wrong." Too often, investors break this rule. They think they can will their stocks to victory somehow, that things will come out well in the end if they just try hard enough. And that's just not how it works.

Businesspeople make the mistake of thinking they can will their ventures to success as well, but in a slightly different way. Rather than getting too emotionally attached to their creations—as I did with my first restaurant—they take a more cerebral, but no less flawed, approach. Most entrepreneurs and corporate executives are, understandably, confident people. They have an unshakable faith in their instincts, their intelligence, and the products or services their companies offer. But, over the years, I've seen this self-assurance blind even the sharpest, most capable managers to a fatal problem: their target customers simply don't want what they're selling.

CLOGGED THINKING

One of the smartest people I have ever met said one of the dumbest things I have ever heard.

He was the CEO of Chemtrak (stock symbol: CMTR), which specialized in take-home medical tests. I drove down to visit the company's headquarters in an office park outside of Palo Alto soon after Chemtrak went public. Chemtrak's only product was an over-the-counter blood test for cholesterol levels. It had just received FDA approval, and Wall Street was all aflutter. CMTR had shot up from $10 to $20 on the news.

The company's chief executive was a lean, dignified-looking man with a graying beard and a beautiful red silk turban wrapped around his head. To demonstrate the ease and usability of Chemtrak's newly approved test, he had his secretary bring one into the office for me to try. She opened the packaging and removed a small plastic lancet, then showed me how to prick my finger with it. I don't normally expect to shed blood at business meetings, but I went ahead and did as she directed.

"It is painless," the CEO reassured me in his lilting Indian accent. "Just a little pinch."

His secretary helped me squeeze a small drop of my blood into a plastic vial that contained a test strip.

"In twelve minutes we will have the results," her boss announced with a proud smile. "It's that easy."

As I placed a small bandage on my finger, I told him that, as easy as the test was to administer, I was skeptical about the hype surrounding the product. It just didn't seem like something American consumers would buy in big numbers. His response shocked me. After giving me a brief but authoritative report on the epidemic levels of heart disease in our country, and how lowering cholesterol levels was a crucial preventive measure, he delivered an astoundingly dense analogy: "Our research indicates that there are five million home pregnancy tests sold every year. Nearly all of those tests are purchased by women. But both men and women in America are concerned about heart health and cholesterol. Therefore, we are confident our sales will exceed five million units per year."

I had to take a moment to process his words. I thought I must have misheard him. This man was not only an accomplished executive, he also had a PhD in, I believe, biochemistry. His IQ was almost certainly a few touchdowns higher than mine. And yet I couldn't deny it: he was making the single most idiotic argument I had ever heard. People buy pregnancy kits because they absolutely *have* to know the results. They're extremely invested in the outcome, to say the least. Somebody who just ate a Big Mac at McDonald's or a Double-Double at In-N-Out Burger does not feel anywhere near that same sense of urgency when it comes to their cholesterol. If anything, cholesterol is the last thing on their mind. They don't want to ruin the pleasure of the meal they've just had by thinking about how bad it was for them. That's just not how American consumers behave. Throw in the fact that Chemtrak's product was a blood test, and the comparison gets even more untenable. There's no way someone's going to rush off to Walgreens or CVS, plunk down twenty bucks, and then *stab themselves in the finger* just so they can feel guilty for overindulging.

The CEO looked a little mystified by my reaction. I'm sure he had delivered this speech to numerous potential investors, and apparently I was the first person to balk at it. Thankfully, my test results were ready by that point, so we could change the subject. As usual, despite my generally atrocious diet, my cholesterol was superbly low. (My wife is always shocked at this, and a little bit jealous.) The CEO congratulated me on my good health and I quickly departed his office.

I was inclined to short Chemtrak's stock right away. I was fairly certain that its take-home cholesterol test would flop. But the fact that such an accomplished scientist and professional was so sure it would succeed scared me, so I decided to do a little more research before I made my decision. I sent a gofer who was working for me at the time to twenty drugstores around my office. I had him put a small nick on the packaging of the first five Chemtrak tests on the shelf at every location. He went back every other week for several months. At the end of this process, those first five tests in all the stores still had nicks on them. Not a single one had sold. That was all the proof I needed. I shorted Chemtrak's stock. It quickly dropped below a dollar. But, as so often happens with failing companies, the company held out for way longer than I expected. Its stock didn't go all the way to zero for another five years.

When I opened a Cajun restaurant in Marin County, I was too emotionally involved in my business. I was so excited to share my favorite food that I couldn't see the plain fact that nobody else in Marin County wanted to eat it. Chemtrak's management was much more cerebral in their approach. They had scientifically analyzed the health-care market and come up with a product they were convinced would fill an important need. The problem was, their analysis was just plain wrong. Even though heart disease is a major problem in this country, American consumers were simply not going to buy what Chemtrak was selling. Lots and lots of very smart people make this mistake. They fixate on some given set of data or analysis instead of the most important data set of all: *how people in the real world behave.* You can know everything there is to know about your industry—market trends, leading indicators, the latest technology—but if you don't know your own customers, you might as well be trying to sell gumbo to gray-haired flower children.

FATHER KNOWS BEST

My dad still lives in my hometown of Tempe, Arizona, but he comes out to visit regularly, especially in the summer months when the temperature in Arizona approaches the surface of your average white dwarf star. He's a retired college professor, and he's always been interested in investing, so sometimes when he's in town, I'll bring him along to meetings with corporate executives. It's a fun way to spend some time together. And I appreciate the company while I'm on the road.

One morning in 1999, we drove across the Golden Gate Bridge and through San Francisco to a business park built on a spit of land, called Oyster Point, that sticks out into the bay. A company called PlanetRx (stock symbol: PLRX) had its headquarters there and I had an appointment with the CFO, a fellow named Steve.

This was during the heyday of the dotcom boom, when everybody and their brother was crowing about things like "the new economy" and predicting the end of brick-and-mortar retail. It was a crazy time, and it brought on the most irrational and inflated asset bubble in the history of capitalism. I'll talk more about that later. For now, I'll stick to my morning with my father and PlanetRx's CFO. Steve invited us into his office overlooking the bay and told us all about how his company was going to remake the drug business the way Amazon.com had remade the book business. Instead of schlepping to the local drugstore, he explained, people would simply log on to PlanetRx's website to order prescriptions and have them delivered straight to their door.

"It's so easy," he boasted as he demonstrated on his laptop. "You can do everything with a few clicks of the mouse."

He then launched into a short presentation of the company's projected earnings. Of course, it was wildly optimistic. PlanetRx was on the verge of "scaling," he claimed, or rapidly growing its revenues. That was the big buzz word at the time. I didn't interrupt him or question his figures. The dotcom mania had been flourishing for three years by then. I was used to those kinds of, shall we say, *enhanced* prognostications. The whole Bay Area economy had blown up bigger than Barry Bonds's hat size. To my surprise, though, my father did clear his throat and chime in with a question.

"Excuse me, sir," he said. "If I were to use your service, how long would it take for my medication to arrive?"

"It depends on where you live," Steve replied. "In most of the country, it'll get there in 24 to 48 hours. For more remote places like Alaska or a small town in South Dakota, it might be more like three days."

"But I can drive down to the local drugstore and get my pills in fifteen minutes," my father countered.

"Maybe so, but with our service, you don't have to leave your house."

"But with your service, I have to wait two days, maybe three!"

They went back and forth like this for a good five or ten minutes. I couldn't believe what was happening. I just sat there with my mouth open and watched my father debate this executive. It was actually quite enjoyable. A lifelong academic, my dad has developed a very strong and finely calibrated BS detector. And as he was discovering in that office on Oyster Point, BS was the chief product of the dotcom industry in the late 1990s. He pointed out to the PlanetRx CFO that the majority of people who used prescription medications were senior citizens like himself.

"By and large, that population isn't very comfortable using the computer to shop," he explained. "Most people in their sixties and seventies don't even know how to do it. How do you expect to make any money when your main customers can't even figure out how to use your service?"

"Easy. We'll teach them. People learned to use Amazon."

"But Amazon sells books. You don't *need* a book. You can wait a few days for it to show up. If you go days without your medicine, you get sick."

"People just have to get used to ordering their refills a little earlier, that's all."

"So you're going to teach your customers to do that, too?" my father pressed him.

Steve pulled at his tie and adjusted his weight in his chair. I decided to let him off the hook and ended the meeting. As my father and I walked through the parking lot to my car, he turned to me and said, "You should keep your eye on that company, son."

"What do you mean?" I asked. "It sounded like you disliked everything about it."

"I did," he replied with a smile. "Except for one thing. The furniture in their offices was much nicer than the stuff in your office. I'll bet you'll be able to buy it for ten cents on the dollar when they go broke."

I never shorted PlanetRx. In those heady days of the dotcom boom, shorting tech stocks was a scary proposition. Just about every company in the industry was enormously overvalued. I knew there was almost certainly a crash coming. It wasn't a question of if, but when. But predicting when exactly when that would arrive was impossible.

I did, however, take my father's advice and keep an eye on PLRX. At the time of our visit, the company had next to nothing in revenues, yet its stock had been flirting with $40 a share. But the high times didn't last long. Even with the dotcom boom still going strong, the company's poor sales started to scare investors. Its stock slowly inched down after our meeting. Then it cratered. In mid-2000, barely a year after my father debated the CFO, PlanetRx laid off a large portion of its staff and moved to Memphis. As we used to say in the business before stocks were listed decimally, the company's stock went "hat-sized," meaning it sold for a fraction of a dollar.

The reason for PlanetRx's demise is quite simple. It only took my father a couple of minutes to spot it. The very consumers the company planned to serve had absolutely no interest in what they were offering. In some ways, PlanetRx failed for the same reason my first restaurant did—its founders confused their own tastes with the tastes of their target market. Like most tech companies, PlanetRx was launched by a bunch of techies who used the internet for just about everything they needed. They assumed that your average grandma and grandpa out in Middle America would share their love for the convenience of online shopping. But, as my dad so astutely pointed out, senior citizens aren't exactly early adopters of technology. More important, the service PlanetRx was offering was actually *less convenient* than the method people were already using! In that regard, PlanetRx was very similar to Chemtrak. Its founders had analyzed their industry. They had come up with all sorts of impressive numbers and projections showing that their product would fill a profitable niche. But, as with Chemtrak's management team, they hadn't analyzed the thing that would make them money: the way people in the real world actually behave.

This failure to account for real-life human behavior also brought down the most overhyped company of the dotcom bubble (besides perhaps the still unbelievable Pets.com), Webvan. If you aren't familiar with the story, Webvan delivered groceries. Despite that modest premise, it managed to raise and then blow hundreds of millions of dollars in a few short years. I was not dumb enough to invest in Webvan. I was even dumber. I invested $50,000 of my own money in a copycat business, a small start-up in Texas called Groceryworks. A buddy of mine pitched me on the company. His main selling point was the long distances between most homes in Texas and the nearest grocery stores. Having lived in Houston, I knew what he was talking about. Sometimes just going out for a gallon of milk felt like a sequel to *On the Road*. I thought people would be willing to pay to avoid that hassle.

I thought wrong.

The shoppers who buy the most groceries have families. They're usually moms, though there are plenty of dads who shop now, too. And for parents, purchasing food is not like purchasing any other product. We're talking about the stuff that sustains and nourishes your children. Making sure that you're getting the best quality merchandise is not just important, it's an instinctual drive. There's no way you're going to trust a website and some kid out in a warehouse somewhere to do it for you. Think about a mother who plans to serve fish for dinner. She has to see that tuna steak or that fillet of salmon. She has to pick it out herself so she can make sure it's the right color and that it doesn't smell like it's been sitting in the display case for a week. If she doesn't do that, she's going to feel like a bad mother. That's not an exaggeration. *It's how people are.* You can't get around human nature no matter how cool and easy-to-use your website is. We're talking about parental instinct here. That's a powerful force. And it completely trumped the benefits of shopping online for groceries.

As with a lot of the stories I share in this book, the flaws in Webvan's and PlanetRx's business models might seem obvious as I write about them. But they couldn't have been that obvious at the time, because a lot of very smart people poured a whole bunch of money into the businesses. When it launched its website, PlanetRx had hundreds of millions in venture capital behind it. At one point, its market capitalization reached into the *billions*. Even after its stock started dropping, there were still plenty of analysts and other experts recommending it virtually up until the day the NASDAQ delisted it. Webvan's early backers included the same people

REDELIVERED

Unlike Webvan, the grocery delivery company I invested in, Groceryworks, didn't go completely under. It was acquired by the supermarket chain Safeway. I received a check for $9,000 after the deal was completed—better than nothing, but less than 20 percent of my original investment. Ouch. The service went on to become a seldom-used perk for the small amount of Safeway's customers who preferred to have their groceries delivered.

Recently, companies like Amazon have gone into the grocery delivery business. But, as with Safeway and Groceryworks, these delivery offerings are ancillary services that will likely never make substantial profits. Most shoppers, especially those with families, still want to inspect the food they buy, and they're simply not going to trust a stranger in a distribution center to choose it for them.

In Amazon's case, its "Fresh" delivery service gives customers the added convenience of adding a couple boxes of cereal and some cans of tuna fish to their orders for other consumer items. But I doubt Jeff Bezos and other Amazon executives are seriously banking on it to bring in real money. Groceries have low margins to begin with, and Amazon is competing with major players like Walmart. If anything, Bezos might see grocery delivery as a loss leader, a way to drive users to Amazon's platform so they'll order more profitable products.

who had funded Apple, Google, and PayPal. And its executives were absolute all-stars. The founder started Borders Books. The CEO came over from Arthur Andersen. These were not dumb or inexperienced people. They were just so caught up in the mania of the dotcom boom and the almost cultlike conviction that the internet would remake every industry that they forgot to think about—or study—*how actual people in the actual world behave.* But this kind of mistake didn't start or end with the tech boom in the 1990s. It happens all the time.

Indeed, *failure is one business trend that never goes out of style.*

FOUR

MADNESS AND MANIAS

Men, it has been well said, think in herds; they go mad in herds, while they recover their senses slowly, one by one.

—Charles MacKay, *Extraordinary Popular Delusions and the Madness of Crowds*

IN MY THIRTY YEARS OF RUNNING MONEY, I'VE LIVED through several historic asset bubbles, otherwise known as manias. I've already recounted some of my experiences during and after the housing craze of the mid-2000s. I also had a front-row seat for the last days of the East Texas oil boom. But nothing compares to the dotcom delirium of the late 1990s. Thinking back on those years is like remembering a weird dream. For half a decade, Silicon Valley turned into nothing less than a business world version of Jonestown. The Kool-Aid wasn't lethal. But it was very potent, and people were drinking it by the gallon.

I remember one particular meeting that captured the mood of the era. In March 2000, I drove to San Mateo to speak with some executives of a website company called Women.com (stock symbol: WOMN). It specialized in content related to, you guessed it, women. Theoretically, the company made money by selling banner ads on its sites. But even after several years in business, no one had figured out how to turn that theory into real-life revenues. Like PlanetRx, Webvan, and just about every other dotcom company at the time, the only thing Women.com excelled at was spending its investors' cash. Of course, that didn't stop its stock price from shooting up way higher than it had any right to.

Women.com's CEO was a petite, fast-talking young professional named Marleen. She showed me a slide deck on her laptop of the company's various web portals. They had sites that dealt with pregnancy, parenting, fashion, cooking, careers, and dozens of other topics—pretty much anything and everything a web-surfing female might be interested in.

"We're one of only two companies in the country targeting this demographic," Marleen explained with a winning smile. "We're extremely well positioned."

She went on to describe that women were the fastest-growing population of internet users and how Women.com intended to continue to appeal to them. Then came the usual preposterously optimistic revenue projections and the mandatory talk of scaling.

When she was finished, I asked her a single question: "If I buy 100,000 shares of your stock tomorrow morning, and a year from now it's lost half its value, why would that have happened?"

"You mean what could go wrong?" Marleen asked.

"Yes."

"Quite frankly, Mr. Fearon," she said, "nothing. We've looked at all the data, and we've discussed this very issue at the board level and we all agree: there's just no way we can lose."

She smiled even more brightly now. I cleared my throat to give her a minute to elaborate, but all she did was continue to grin.

"So you're saying there is no chance that anything will go wrong for your company in the next year?"

"That is exactly what I'm saying," she beamed. "We're going to have an incredible year. And the year after that will be even better."

At the time, a share of WOMN was trading for around $15. Ten months later, it was about 70 cents. Before a full year had elapsed after my meeting with Marleen, Women.com had ceased to exist. It was bought out for pennies a share by its chief rival, a company called iVillage (stock symbol: IVIL), which was also circling the drain. iVillage's descent had been even more dramatic. Its stock broke the $100 mark at the height of the boom. By the time it acquired Women.com, you could buy a share of IVIL for less than two bucks.*

Not everyone in Silicon Valley got caught up in the hysteria. My good friend Bandel Carano is a long-standing investor in my fund. Bandel's the senior partner at a venture capital firm in Palo Alto called Oak Investments. He's one of the shrewdest evaluators of start-ups in the country. For the last twenty years, we've been meeting for lunch twice a year down on Woodside Road, either at Buck's or the Village Pub. At one of these lunches in the late 1990s, Bandel was beside himself.

"None of these companies are ever going to make any money, Scott," he told me as we ate our salads. "But people just keep pouring capital into them."

He ticked off a dozen names of now-infamous dotcom busts that were, at the time, swimming in venture capital money. One of the companies he mentioned was Webvan, which really got Bandel's blood up. He and the other guys at Oak had passed on funding it early on. But just

---

*Betsy Schiffman, "iVillage Swallows Women.com," *Forbes,* February 6, 2001.

about every other VC firm in the valley was writing seven-, eight-, even nine-figure checks for it.

"It wasn't a hard decision for us to say no," Bandel said. "It was easy. We studied their proposal and right away we knew there was no way they would turn a profit in a million years. None. It was *obvious*. I don't know what kind of math people are using anymore, but it's not the math I learned in school."

This is what happens in manias. People willfully forget inconvenient facts like arithmetic. Alan Greenspan famously called this phenomenon irrational exuberance, but that was a major understatement. Remember when I said that Costco's multiple (the ratio of its share price to its earnings per share) scared me away from buying the stock? It was in the thirties. Dotcoms like Webvan and Women.com had *infinitely* higher multiples than that because they had *no* earnings. But investors were so hot to believe in these companies—and the great new internet age—that they started valuing them based on page views, or "eyeballs," as they called it. No, I am not kidding.

I still have a research report from the brokerage Credit Suisse First Boston on a company called Commerce One. "Conventional valuation measures," the report says, "don't capture a revenue stream where the real value is hidden in services yet to be introduced."*

That report is from late 1999. I've read it dozens of times since then, and I still don't understand what they were saying. "Services yet to be introduced"? Huh? But this kind of gobbledygook was *everywhere* at the time. One analyst at Paine Webber tried to talk me out of shorting a

---

*David Shabelman, "Net Stocks Treading Water Along with Broader Market," *The Street.com*, September 13, 1999.

money-losing dotcom by repeatedly predicting a price target based on something called its "future terminal multiple." When I finally asked him what the hell that term even meant, it turned out he had made it up.

These methods of hyping dubious investment (Commerce One filed for bankruptcy in 2004) were certainly "irrational." But I wouldn't say they were based on mere "exuberance." Once you start making up new ways to value companies based on fantasy scenarios ten years down the road, you're not just being exuberant. You might as well start measuring your head for a shiny new tinfoil hat, because you've officially crossed over into an alternate universe. And yet most people in the valley thought Bandel and I were the crazy ones for being skeptical of this nonsense.

SUNK

One month after my visit to Women.com, I parked my car on Brannan Street in the South of Market neighborhood of San Francisco and strolled into the corporate headquarters of a company called Quokka Sports (stock symbol: QKKA). Its CEO was a youthful, energetic Aussie named Alan. He had curly blond hair, brilliant white teeth, and an unusual idea for the next big thing in sports broadcasting.

"Yacht racing!" he declared to me as I sat down in his office.

"Yacht racing?" I asked. "You mean, like a bunch of rich guys sipping champagne on a sailboat? That kind of thing?"

"No, mate!" he laughed. "I mean teams of highly skilled athletes competing in one of the most exciting sports in the world. Let me show you."

Alan fired up the iMac on his desk and logged on to Quokka's website. It showed a sailboat lowering its jib. A couple of other sailboats were behind it. I surmised that they were in some kind of race. But it was hard to be sure. They were hundreds of feet from each other and they looked like they were going about three miles an hour.

"Is this in slow motion?" I asked.

"No," Alan replied with a frown. "This is live. Check this out."

He clicked his mouse and the action—if you can call it that—switched over to a close-up of a crew member on one of the boats turning some kind of spinning handle. (I'm sure the thing has a special nautical name, but like most Americans, I don't know a thing about sailing.) Alan clicked his mouse again, and the screen switched over in quick succession to the view at the top of the boat's mast, then behind the helm, then alongside the hull, almost down at the waterline. The last camera angle Alan showed me was from a buoy. As the thing heaved up and down in the waves, the first sailboat passed close by and started to turn. I had to look away. I was getting seasick.

"We call it *immersive viewing*," Alan enthused. "You can choose which camera you want to watch at any given time. It puts you right in the action!"

For the next few minutes, he explained that the America's Cup race was about to start down in Australia and boasted that Quokka had secured the exclusive online rights to the broadcast. To be honest, I wasn't paying very close attention at that point. I was still a little queasy. Then Alan said something that piqued my interest: "We expect a minimum of two million unique visitors to our site during the race."

"Two million visitors?" I asked. "You mean, worldwide?"

"No, in America. Worldwide we expect double that amount."

"I don't know about the rest of the world," I said. "But do you really think Americans will get excited about *sailboats?*"

"Absolutely!" Alan cried. "When they get to witness them up close like this, they will."

As a rule, I don't get into debates with executives. That's not why I go to these meetings. But this argument was so farfetched, I had to challenge it. "Alan, I'll bet only one out of a thousand people in California has ever even been on a sailboat. And if you're talking about the rest of the country, it's probably more like one out of every *fifty* thousand, maybe even less. Why would they care about the America's Cup?"

"Because watching it online will change everything, Scott. They can see every angle! They can create their own experience!"

As I said in the last chapter, I was extremely gun-shy when it came to shorting tech stocks during the dotcom boom. That caution kept me from shorting Women.com and PlanetRx. But not Quokka. Almost exactly one year after my meeting with Alan, the company filed for bankruptcy.

I forgot to mention that during our meeting, Alan looked like he had just stepped off a yacht himself, right down to the Sperry Top-Siders he was wearing sans socks and the knit sweater he had cinched loosely around his neck. It turned out, he was an avid sailor. He had even worked for the Australian team in an earlier America's Cup. In other words, his enthusiasm for yacht racing was a classic case of a businessman confusing his own tastes for the tastes of his target market, just like I did when I opened a Cajun restaurant in Marin County, California. But I didn't include the story of Quokka Sports in that earlier chapter because, to my mind, it's an even better example of what manias do to people's brains.

At their core, manias are about storytelling. People become enchanted with a story, and they convince themselves—and each other—that it just *has* to be true no matter what. During the dotcom era, people fell in love with a story about the internet: that it would magically transform human behavior. I can't think of a stronger illustration of this than Alan's predictions about yachting. He thought that just because Quokka planned to show the America's Cup online, average Americans would suddenly give a damn about it. Think about that for a moment. He had so much faith in the internet's power, he expected it to make a nation of NASCAR fans log on to watch a bunch of billionaires bobbing around in the middle of the ocean.

The oil boom that I lived through in Houston was predicated on an equally fictitious story: that the price of crude would rise forever. The same was true for the real estate bubble of the mid-2000s. People invested everything, not just their money but their hopes and dreams, in what amounted to a very dangerous fairy tale: that their houses would always be worth more and more and more. In many ways, mania participants suffer from acute cases of historical myopia. They only look as far back as the first days of their particular bubble and assume that older ways of living or doing business have now been rendered permanently obsolete. This was especially true during the dotcom boom, when people who seemed perfectly reasonable would stop you on the street and tell you that the "new economy" of the internet had made investing metrics such as profit margins—or even actual revenues—relics of a bygone age.

It's easy to look back at manias in the past and spot the central flaws in peoples' reasoning. But, trust me, *manias happen all the time.* There are probably several of them taking place as you read this. They might not be as big or historic as the ones I have discussed so far. They might even be limited to individual industries. Barely a decade after the dotcom crash, people in Silicon Valley and the Bay Area tech world as a whole started to party, to paraphrase Prince, like it was 1999 all over again. Even after the harsh lessons of the first bubble, venture capitalists and

SUNK, PART II

Manias don't die easily, especially when they're fueled by rich, powerful, and obsessive people. In 2013, fourteen years after Alan swore that "immersive viewing" would magically cause Americans to love sailing, Oracle founder Larry Ellison tried to bring yachting to the masses again when he hosted the America's Cup on San Francisco Bay.

Ellison made many of the same claims the CEO of Quokka Sports had tried out on me more than a decade earlier—specifically, that people would suddenly care about a bunch of billionaires on sailboats if they could see the action up close. Promising that the races would attract huge influxes of visitors and over a billion dollars in economic benefits (three times as much as the Super Bowl!), he convinced San Francisco's political leaders to spend millions in public money on waterfront facilities and viewing areas. Ellison even managed to get NBC Sports to broadcast the event. But, just like Quokka Sports, his efforts were a bust.

Thanks to Ellison's insistence on using cutting-edge, massively expensive catamarans, only four teams could afford to enter the competition. Because of the small number of challengers, several of the preliminary rounds featured the bizarre spectacle of one boat racing itself around the bay. Making matters worse, a crew member on one of those teams died tragically during a practice session, so organizers imposed strict limits on wind conditions, which caused frequent race cancellations.

A fair number of people did turn out to watch some of the races, especially on weekends. I have to admit, those space-age catamarans were pretty cool looking, and I even drove down to the city one day to see them for myself. But more often than not, the stands along the shore of the bay were empty. Television ratings were surprisingly high for the opening day of the main event, but they quickly dipped close to the levels of another sport Americans have a history of ignoring: soccer.*

*Richard Sandomir, "NBC Gets More Than It Expected," *New York Times*, September 25, 2013.

larger corporations began to throw huge piles of money at every start-up with a half-baked smartphone app. In 2013, the founders of Snapchat— an application mostly used by teenagers to send goofy photos to each other—turned down a $3 billion buyout offer from Facebook. I don't know what's more maniacal: that one company offered that kind of cash for the rights to an obscure product or that the other said no to it. Another sector that has behaved maniacally for years is renewable energy. Replacing dirty carbon-based fuels is a laudable and critically important goal. But too often, businesspeople, investors, and consumers buy into unrealistic technologies with little or no chance of making a short-term profit, let alone revolutionizing the world's energy consumption. A few years ago, investors would rain money on any company that had anything to do with biofuels such as ethanol. The same thing happened with hydrogen fuel cells, then solar, wind, and other green sources. I'm not claiming that these technologies are worthless, just that the enthusiasm for them often seems awfully, well, *exuberant*.

Manias can even take hold at individual companies. Managements—and investors—willfully believe all of the happy parts of a given narrative about their firms and ignore gaping flaws in their reasoning. I once visited the offices of a hot new chain of cafeteria-style, all-you-can-eat restaurants called Fresh Choice (stock symbol: SALD). It had just come public a few months earlier, and its stock had already almost doubled. Everyone who worked there was dressed straight out of a J.Crew catalog: below-the-knees skirts, tucked shirts, pressed trousers. And everyone—and I mean *everyone*—smiled and said hello to me as I walked by. It was the friendliest corporate environment I've ever been in. For a minute I thought I had woken up in the movie *Pleasantville*.

The two executives I met, the company's CEO and CFO, were as inviting and genial as their employees. They were young guys in their early forties, very clean-cut and well groomed, and they came striding out of their offices with giant grins on their faces. To hear them talk, they had good reason to be so happy. They were going to revolutionize their entire industry.

"There's no way a mother or a father would bring their children to most restaurants if they knew what they were serving," the CEO said. "The kitchens are filthy, the food is old and frozen and barely warmed over. But we're different. For a reasonable price, you can bring your family to Fresh Choice and know that they're going to get nutritious food that was prepared the same day."

He then talked at length and in exhaustive detail about how clean Fresh Choice locations were—everything from how often the employees were required to scrub the kitchens and serving areas to how they maintained the refrigeration units beneath the salad bars to the special type of scraping tools they used to clean off the counters. I think he even described the types of muffins they served and how often they baked them. Most of all, he emphasized the importance of appealing to families. He must have said the word *family* fifty times in less than an hour. According to him, giving families a low-priced, high-quality option for eating out was going to make Fresh Choice the king of chain restaurants.

I was so struck by his zeal for healthy, clean, and inexpensive dining that when I got home I did a little research on him. I discovered that he and most of the other executives in the company were Mormons. It all made sense to me then—the Donnie-and-Marie friendliness, the J.Crew wardrobes, and, most of all, the obsessive focus on creating a family atmosphere in their restaurants. Big families are the norm in Mormon culture. And even for the fairly well off, taking a big family out to eat can be prohibitively expensive. It was plain what the Fresh Choice guys were after: they were trying to give people like themselves a chance to enjoy a meal with their kids without having to dip into their college funds to afford it.

Unlike my experience with my own restaurant, I quickly saw Fresh Choice's fundamental error: the very customers they were trying to reach didn't want what they wanted. Most Fresh Choice locations were in the Bay Area. By and large in that market, and in other big cities like Los Angeles and New York, the people who care about eating quality food are not going to go to a place that looks like a cafeteria—not even a sparkling clean cafeteria. Pushing a tray down a counter is just not their idea of a great dining experience. They're willing to pay extra to be waited on. On the other hand, most of the people that do go for the all-you-can-eat concept aren't interested in how nutritious the food is or how immaculate the countertops are. They want their fare cheap, filling, and plentiful—and they want meatloaf and chicken fried steak, not Greek salads and pasta primavera.

Investors bought into Fresh Choice's vision for spotlessly clean, cafeteria-style dining for a little while. Like I said, it only took a couple months for its stock to double after its initial public offering. The company rode that momentum and expanded rapidly, opening outlets on the East Coast and in the South. But the good times didn't last. After a few years, Fresh Choice smelled pretty stale. Same-store sales fell, they started closing locations, and its stock slid down into single digits. Bankruptcy didn't come for another several years, but it was only a matter of time.

No matter their scale or their origins, the same dynamics are at play in all manias: people get so caught up in a compelling story, they convince themselves and each other that it is destined to come true. Like Marleen at Women.com or the founders of Fresh Choice, they think there is no way they can fail. That is a very dangerous mind-set, because *believing that you can't fail is one of the best ways to do just that.*

SWEATING IT OUT

One of the more maniacal industries in the last thirty years has been biotech. I've seen dozens of companies in that sector come public—and soar to huge valuations—on nothing more than a few promising results in the lab. The founders of a company down in Redwood City called Cygnus Therapeutics (stock symbol: CYGN) had a particularly hopeful story. Way back in the early 1990s, they announced that they were going to manufacture a noninvasive method for monitoring glucose levels in the blood. They called their product the GlucoWatch. It was exactly what it sounds like—a wristwatch that gave regular readouts of its wearer's blood sugar levels. Amazingly, Cygnus claimed its invention wouldn't need to draw any blood to accomplish this. It would detect glucose in a person's sweat.

As you can imagine, the GlucoWatch promised to be a huge benefit for anyone with diabetes. Instead of having to draw their own blood, diabetics could simply glance at their wrists every so often. The watch even featured alarms that would alert users if their glucose levels reached a dangerous level. That's not just an added convenience; that's a potentially lifesaving technology. Needless to say, investors, including me, were *very* interested in Cygnus's progress in developing the watch. With more and more Americans being diagnosed with diabetes every year, it had a chance to be a blockbuster, Prozac-level product.

Cygnus's offices were in a business park east of the 101 freeway between a granite quarry and a go-kart track. Interestingly, it shared a parking lot with NeXT Computer, the company Steve Jobs started after he was booted from Apple. I was at Cygnus a total of five times between 1994 and 2002. It's rare that I visit a company that often if I don't own its stock. But I was excited by Cygnus's idea and I wanted to keep up with how it was faring.

Every time I went down there, I got the same story from the various executives I met with: the watch was *almost* ready. The only thing that changed was the reasons for the delay. They were working through the last technical challenges, they were dealing with regulatory obstacles, they were finalizing testing procedures. There was never a doubt about the final chapter to the story, though: the watch was going to be a huge success. The brass at Cygnus was so confident, they sold the rights to other products they were developing so they could pour everything they had into bringing the watch to market.*

At one of these meetings, the company's chief operating officer, a Stanford MBA named Craig, strapped a prototype watch to my wrist. While Craig was giving me the latest rundown about why the watch wasn't quite ready for mass production yet, I waited to find out what my glucose levels were—and waited and waited some more. After fifteen minutes, the prototype was still blinking double zeroes at me. I figured my wrist wasn't sweaty enough for it to get a reading, so I started shaking my arm around to get it to perspire. That was not a good plan. I accidentally rapped the edge of the conference table and cracked the face of the watch. For a second, I was terrified that I had ruined the company's one and only model. I could see the headlines in my mind: "Hedge Fund Manager Destroys Million-Dollar Prototype!" But Craig was a good sport about it. He assured me they had dozens of others. He even offered to get another one for me to try, but I declined. I didn't want to take the risk. I sat very still for the rest of his presentation.

Looking back, that incident was definitely an omen. The whole idea of the GlucoWatch was, well, cracked. As it turned out, there was a very good reason it took Cygnus so long to develop the watch: getting accurate blood sugar levels out of perspiration is incredibly hard, maybe even impossible (though some companies are still working on it today). After years and years of development, Cygnus finally managed to get FDA approval for their first version of the product in 2001. But it didn't come close to living up to expectations. The first GlucoWatch quickly earned

---

*"Cygnus Sells Drug-Delivery Assets," *Silicon Valley Business Journal,* November 19, 1999.

a bad reputation for producing faulty readings. Not only that, it gave a lot of people nasty rashes on their wrists. As a result, sales were sluggish. That didn't deter Cygnus, though. It put out a second-generation watch the following year, and it was just as flawed as the first. By then, the company's stock was trading in the pennies. The rest of the world had figured out what Craig and the other guys at Cygnus still couldn't face: that the story they had been telling themselves and others simply wasn't true. As hopeful as the GlucoWatch was, it just plain didn't work. And since they had sold the rights to other products they had been working on, Cygnus was nothing but a one-trick pony—and that pony was dead.

I was sad to see Cygnus fail, and not just because I wanted to buy truckloads of its stock and make a fortune when it succeeded. I don't normally get emotionally involved in the companies I research. And it's not like I shed any tears over Cygnus's demise. But I could definitely understand why the people working there believed so fervently in the dream of the GlucoWatch. It was the complete opposite of Chemtrak's cholesterol test. That was a case of businessmen pushing an invasive product that consumers didn't want, let alone need. The GlucoWatch, on the other hand, could have been a lifesaving device that actually spared millions of people from the invasive procedure of drawing blood. But the fact remains: the thing was a dud—and so Cygnus, for all its promise, crashed just as hard as Chemtrak.

The whole concept of reading glucose levels in perspiration was probably doomed from the start. But rather than face this disappointing reality, Cygnus's executives tried even harder to make it work. They even sold off other assets so that they could continue to squander their money on it. This behavior reminds me of a common mistake investors make: buying a stock as it drops. It's called *averaging down.* You see it all the time, even from seasoned pros. They believe in a certain company. They think it is destined for greatness. And they get so infatuated with that positive narrative that when things don't work out the way they expected and the company's stock starts to fall, they actually buy more of it. Perversely, they convince themselves that it's a *good* thing that the stock is dropping because that means they can get more shares for a better price. They keep reassuring themselves with this flawed reasoning right up until the day they go broke.

This is such a common mistake, there's even a Wall Street saying for it: "Double-up, triple-up, belly-up." Short-sellers do it, too, but in reverse. They short more of a company's stock as it rises, all the while telling themselves that they'll wind up making more when it drops. But they rarely survive long enough to see that happen.

Like I've said, the best money managers are also the best quitters. They quit early and they quit often. As soon as they see things turning for the worse, they don't wait around, they bail. This same quality is just as important in business. That's not to say that tenaciousness isn't important or that faith in your abilities and your ideas is a bad thing somehow. But you have to separate faith from *blind* faith. Cygnus's leaders put years and years, not to mention every cent they had, into what was almost certainly a lost cause. Instead of adapting their approach to deal with that very strong possibility, they doubled and tripled up. The result was all too predictable.

Speaking of blind faith, for more than a decade, a company called Shaman Pharmaceuticals (stock symbol: SHMN) managed to get by on little else. In all that time, it never produced a single revenue-generating medicine. But the power of its story was enough to bring in hundreds of millions of dollars in stock offerings and private investments.

The founder and CEO of Shaman, a woman named Lisa, could certainly cast a spell. She had long cinnamon-colored hair and striking brown eyes. I went to visit her in Shaman's offices down by the San Francisco airport in 1998. Even though she'd been running the company for nine years by then, she was still quite young. I don't think she was even forty yet. And she brimmed with positive energy as she dimmed the lights and gave me a presentation on Shaman's work. She showed me slide after slide of herself and other Shaman employees trekking through the jungles of Brazil, speaking with indigenous people, and collecting samples of plants and trees.

"The rainforests of Brazil contain tens of thousands of undiscovered medicinal compounds," Lisa explained. "We consult with traditional healers from remote tribes to learn how they treat illnesses. Then we bring the plants and herbs they use back to our labs and create pharmaceutical-grade drugs out of them. It's the perfect blend of East and West, old and new."

I must admit, I was quite intrigued by the story and by Lisa's charismatic way of presenting it. There was something about her that made you root for her to succeed. Then I remembered reality: Lisa and the rest of Shaman's executives were well on their way to bankruptcy. They had started out in 1989 with plans to cure major diseases like cancer and HIV. But by the time I visited their offices, they had managed to produce exactly one potential product—an antidiarrheal medication derived from the gooey red secretions of a certain tree in the Amazon—and even that hadn't cleared clinical trials.* As a result, the company's debt was

---

*Amazingly, the drug eventually did gain FDA approval—in 2013, well over a decade after the initial incarnation of Shaman went bankrupt.

mounting at the same time its stock price was starting to drop. In other words, despite Shaman's hopeful premise, it was just another failing company. The year after I met with Lisa, Shaman filed for bankruptcy and SHMN officially went to zero.

The reason why Lisa and Shaman were able to survive for so long and raise so much money without any results is that she was telling a great story, a story that a lot of investors wanted to believe in. Most people don't want to accept corporate-driven solutions to our problems. They don't like the fact that we need Big Oil to find our gas for us or that we need Big Government to run our country. And they are reluctant to acknowledge that Western medicine and Big Pharma, for all of their faults, have lengthened our lifespans and vastly improved the quality of our lives. Lisa offered people an alternative vision. She gave them the (probably false) hope that we could heal ourselves by listening to smaller, simpler societies and rediscovering their forgotten wisdom. It was a nice idea. But in the end, it was little more than a pipe dream.

I want to make one thing clear: Lisa is not a scam artist. She genuinely believed (and still believes) in what she was doing, and she backed up that belief by hiring some of the best biologists and chemists in the country to try to make Shaman's story come true. Amazingly, her dream did not die when the company went into bankruptcy. Lisa started Shaman *Botanicals* and raised millions more in investments to market its antidiarrheal medicine as a dietary supplement. (This allowed the company to bypass the FDA approval process.) Even when this failed, she was not deterred. She formed another company based on the same premise. She even brought it public in London. In 2010, *Forbes* published a feature on her then twenty-year quest to make drugs out of rainforest plants. All told, according to that article, she had raised and spent more than $200 million on the effort.*

From my meeting with Lisa, I know she's a great saleswoman. But after two decades and almost a quarter *billion* dollars, it's incredible to me that investors are still willing to fund her work. And yet the power of her vision and her story seems to blind them to reality. That's what I mean when I say that manias happen all the time, even on very small scales. Whether it's a massive, society-wide bubble like the dotcom boom or individual ventures like Shaman or Cygnus, this same maniacal faith is at work. People get so caught up in an enchanting narrative, they block out any evidence that it might not be true. They refuse to believe that it can fail—sometimes even after it has already failed multiple times.

RUNNING THE OPTION

Luckily for me, I learned very early on how destructive maniacal thinking can be. Living through the Great Texas Oil Bust wasn't my first experience with a financial meltdown. I had a much smaller and much more personal experience with failure a few years earlier, and it helped shape me almost as much as my time in Houston.

Sometime during my freshman year at Stanford, I read a magazine article about options trading. I don't remember where I read it, or why exactly it got me so fired up, but I came back to my hometown of Tempe, Arizona, that summer hot to try my hand at the options game. The lure of it probably had something to do with the fact that, using

*Helen Coster, "One Pharma Entrepreneur's Never Ending Quest," *Forbes,* December 30, 2010.

SNAKE OIL

As I just said, I do not believe that Lisa is a fraud. When you get down to it, Shaman and her subsequent ventures were just plain old failures, like the vast majority of the other companies I write about in this book. But when it comes to the wider alternative health products industry, I'm afraid Lisa is one of the few honest—if misguided—brokers.

In 1993, I paid a visit to Herbalife (stock symbol: HLF), the granddaddy of multilevel marketing, or MLM, companies. Most MLM outfits, like Herbalife, are in the vitamin or natural remedy business. A large amount of them are based in Utah, which has led some people to offer a new meaning for the MLM acronym: Mormons Losing Money. Herbalife's headquarters are not in Utah, though. At the time of my visit, they were in a shiny glass high-rise off the 405 freeway in Los Angeles, directly beneath the flight path of LAX. The COO, a man named Norm, led me into his office and regaled me with the company's plans to expand aggressively into Asia and eastern Europe. Every three minutes or so, the whole building would shake as a jumbo jet thundered past overhead, forcing him to shout.

When he had finished his presentation, I abruptly changed the subject from the company's business plans to something much more important to me—what Herbalife actually put in its products. It was notoriously secretive about how it made its nutrition and weight-loss pills and elixirs. It had also been the subject of multiple investigations by state and federal authorities for false claims and potentially harmful side effects. I didn't bring it up at the time, but to me its new emphasis on foreign markets didn't look so much like an expansion as an evasion, a search for less restrictive regulatory environments and fresh suckers to buy its dubious wares.

"Norm, will Herbalife ever release the ingredients for your products?"

You would have thought I had asked Norm to release naked pictures of his wife. His back stiffened and he gave me a very sour look. The formulas, he declared, were "proprietary."

"But if nobody knows what's in your products, how can investors like me be sure they work?"

The question seemed to take Norm by surprise. I honestly don't think he had ever thought about this issue or at least been asked about it in meetings with potential investors. The only thing he expected me to be interested in was how the company planned to grow revenues. The idea that a money manager would care whether Herbalife's products actually did what they said they did was a shock to him. After a short moment of throat clearing and awkward silence, he came up with a response.

"The best proof that our products work is our founder, Mark Hughes," Norm said. "Before he started this company, he was terribly overweight. Now look at him. He's lean and muscular, the picture of health, all thanks to Herbalife."

I left Herbalife HQ convinced they were nothing but a global, modern-day snake oil business. I didn't short its stock, though, because I knew the alternative health-care mania wasn't going to die anytime soon. Over twenty years later, it still hasn't. A few years ago, hedge fund manager Bill Ackman shorted $1 billion of Herbalife's stock. He accused the company of running a pyramid scheme and mounted an aggressive public relations campaign to bring it down. But, as of this writing, it's still very much alive. Unfortunately, the same can't be said for the company's founder, Mr. Hughes, the man Norm held up as living proof of the benefits of Herbalife's product line. He died in 2000 at the ripe old age of forty-four. His fourth wife found him unconscious after a party in his palatial Malibu mansion. Turns out, he was a tad less health-conscious than he had led his employees to believe. His blood alcohol level was just shy of moonshine. The much advertised mood-enhancing properties of his products obviously didn't help Mark much, either. His autopsy revealed large amounts of pre-scription antidepressants in his system.*

---

*"Binge Led to Death of Herbalife Founder," *New York Times,* August 12, 2000.

options, you can invest in companies for a fraction of the cost of actually buying shares in them. That was quite attractive to my eighteen-year-old mind.

My first week of summer vacation, my father agreed to loan me $500, and I opened an account at a Merrill Lynch office in a strip mall on the corner of North Scottsdale and Camelback roads. I had a job working nights as a bellhop at the Tempe Holiday Inn, which was down the street from the brokerage. I would stop in on my way to the hotel a few times a week, watch the ticker for a little while, and make some trades. I was buying and selling "calls," options to buy stocks at certain prices. It was a lot of fun, but I didn't take it too seriously that first summer. It was just something to do. I especially liked hanging out and talking shop with my broker, a good-natured, middle-aged divorcé named Mike.

Once a week or so when I had a day off, Mike and I would go down to a nearby pizza place after the markets closed. We'd each order a large pizza and pitcher of beer (the drinking age in Arizona was only eighteen). We'd munch on our pizza, drink our beer straight from our pitchers, and converse endlessly about the markets—the hottest stocks, the latest earnings forecasts, trends, rumors, anything and everything having to do with "The Street." I loved those pizza- and beer-fueled gab sessions. They made me feel like a real-live money man. Not only that, it seemed like I had a talent for options trading. By the end of that first summer I had managed to double my dad's initial loan. I flew back for my sopho-more year at Stanford with a cool thousand bucks sitting in my brokerage account.

The following summer, things started out great. I returned to Ari-zona from Palo Alto, and my father not only let me keep the money he'd loaned me the summer before, he matched the amount already in my ac-count. That meant I had a whopping $2,000 to play with, a princely sum to me at the time. My first day in Tempe, I drove up to the Merrill Lynch branch on Camelback Road and started swapping calls again. Mike was pleased to see me and excited to help me continue my winning streak. For the rest of the summer, I stopped in every day on my way to work to confer with him and make my trades. We also resumed our once-a-week pizza-and-beer strategy sessions. I was far more active that second summer. This was not a mere hobby anymore or a summer diversion. This was bordering on an obsession. I hung on every tidbit and rumor Mike passed along. I put everything I had into the effort.

And it was all in vain.

By the end of that second summer, my Merrill Lynch account had exactly zero dollars in it. I'd lost everything—not only the money I'd made the summer before, but the original $500 my father had loaned me and the additional thousand he'd given me, too.

You'd think this experience would have soured me on playing the markets. But it actually made me more interested in them. I never traded options again, but my own personal boom-and-bust left me fascinated by the size, complexity, and dynamism of the financial world. When I got back to Stanford for my junior year, I took more classes on investing and finance, and I decided that I would get an MBA immediately after I graduated. In many ways, losing all that money actually wound up directing me toward my career in money management. I was determined to figure out why I had failed and how I could do better in the future. And I gleaned a few very important lessons from my short and disastrous stint as an options trader:

First: *Stockbrokers are useless.* Nothing against my old pal Mike, but like most of his colleagues in the business, he had very little to offer besides the same old conventional wisdom that everyone else was reading in *Barron's* or the *Wall Street Journal*.

This kind of groupthink is rampant in the financial world. After the fact, I learned that all the hot tips Mike the "Financial Executive" (as his business card described him) had passed along to me were drawn from stuff he was reading in the mass media and hearing from his pals in the industry, who were only parroting other stuff *they* had read in the mass media and heard from *their* pals in the industry. None of them were sharing anything new or especially insightful. They were just repeating the same stale news that everyone else already knew. You can imagine just how stale Mike's so-called expert advice was by the time it traveled all the way out to Tempe, Arizona. This was long before the internet, so I was trading on information that might as well have arrived by Pony Express.

Second: *Trading on trends is a fool's game.* That second summer, with Mike's help, I studied every chart I could find looking for things like "pivots" and "indicators." I might as well have been trying to glean stock tips from my optometrist's eye chart, because it was about as useful as any graph put out by the most prominent Wall Street trend analysts.

Third: *Stocks tend to go up gradually but often go down rapidly.* Traders have a less delicate way of expressing this: "Stocks," they say, "eat like a bird but crap like a bear." I was mainly trading so-called out-of-the-money calls during those summers. By buying these types of options, I was betting on certain stocks to go up in value before the option expiration date. Many did, but not by very much. The stocks that fell were often a much different story. A good number dropped like cartoon anvils, plummeting 10, 20, 30 percent or more in a single trading day. Those experiences left a strong impression on me. There's nothing quite like seeing a stock you're hoping will rise puke up a third of its value right in front of your eyes.

At the time, if someone had asked me to explain what shorts were, I would have held up a pair of swimming trunks. But a few years later, when I learned that you could make money on falling stocks, those hot summer days in the Merrill Lynch office came back to me and helped me realize just how profitable short selling could be.

The fourth and final lesson I took from my options washout was the most important one of all, because it's helped keep me from getting caught up in all the maniacal asset bubbles I've lived through since those early days in Tempe: *effective money managers do not go with the flow.* They are loners, by and large. They're not joiners; they're skeptics, cynics even. Whatever label you want to put on them, the trait they all share is that *they don't automatically trust that what the majority of people—especially the experts—are doing is necessarily correct or wise.* If anything, they move in the opposite direction of the majority, or they at least seek out their own course.

Warren Buffett is the best example of this contrarian impulse. In the 1960s, when Buffett started out, most money managers were investing in highly cyclical, heavily indebted and capital-intensive industrial giants like U.S. Steel. As a consequence, stocks in those kinds of companies were extremely overpriced in Buffett's view, especially when compared to their earnings. Instead of following the majority and buying into that minibubble, he consciously sought out companies on the other end of the spectrum—businesses with lower capital expenditures and higher profit margins—and he wound up buying relatively cheap stocks in ad agencies and regional media companies like Capital Cities, Gannett, and the *Washington Post.* This was a complete departure from the consensus of the time, and it made Buffett a ridiculous amount of money.

My investment focus on dead companies walking also started out as a contrarian idea. When I first came back to California and was running mutual funds for GT Capital, I joined a dinner group with a bunch of other money managers. Every month, we'd all go out for a meal and talk shop. One night, about ten of us went to Il Fornaio down on the Embarcadero in San Francisco. A man named Gary Smith stood up after our plates were cleared and handed around some papers he'd copied for us. He was a former basketball player, at least six foot three, so when he got up from his chair, it was hard not to notice. We all quit talking and listened.

"These are some numbers for Prime Motor Inns," he announced. "They're going broke, boys. Their stock is going to flat-line. And I'm going to make a killing when it does."

The way the rest of the guys reacted, you'd think Gary had just told them the chef had stuffed their raviolis with horse meat. There was a long silence. Nobody knew what to say. Back in those days, what Gary was proposing—shorting a company and hoping it went bankrupt—was very radical. Traders shorted stocks, sure. But most did so infrequently, and when they did, they almost always followed a formula called valuation-based shorting. They'd find a stock with a big price-earnings ratio and go against it until its share price dropped a couple of bucks, then they'd quickly take their profits. What Gary was talking about was a major departure from that strategy. And while everyone else around the table looked perplexed, even horrified, by the idea, I immediately saw the genius of it.

Prime Motor Inns owned most of the Howard Johnson motel and restaurant chain, as well as other hospitality companies. The night of that dinner, its stock was still trading for around $17 a share, and I think it's safe to say that nobody except Gary Smith expected it to go anywhere near zero. I myself had a soft spot for Howard Johnson. When I was a kid, my dad would take my brother and me out to eat at one of their locations across the street from Arizona State University. He and my brother

INCURIOUS

There's no one method or approach that makes for a successful investor. But there is one common trait that I believe all great investors share: intellectual curiosity. Good money managers are broad-minded and intellectually curious. They don't, no, they *can't* just accept conventional wisdom. They are vociferous readers. They crave new ideas and when they hear them, they're willing to try them out. They're not afraid of something just because it's novel or disruptive. In fact, the more iconoclastic an idea is, the more curious they are about it. Unfortunately, this attitude is exceedingly rare on Wall Street.

I used to play a stock-picking game with about twenty different brokerage salesmen and Wall Street analysts. Most of them worked at well-known firms—Merrill Lynch, Alex Brown, Goldman Sachs, Bear Stearns. The rules of the game were simple: pick two longs and one short. You could only swap out picks at the end of each quarter. At the end of one year I mailed a gift to all the participants, a short but insightful book titled *In the Shadows of Wall Street*. Written by Cornell professor Paul Strebel, it analyzed how smaller-company stocks neglected by Wall Street often outperformed those rated as buys. Over the next few months, I asked each of my fellow game participants, one by one, what they'd thought of the book. Not a single one had read beyond the first page.

would always order the fried clams. I would get a hot dog. But by the late 1980s, the brand was definitely looking musty. The company had bought up a bunch of competitors to try to get some of its mojo back, but, as Gary explained that night, those new companies only wound up adding to Prime Motor Inns' problems. It was well over $500 million in debt. At the same time, its revenues were shrinking. Put those two factors together—growing debt and dwindling cash—and you almost always get one result: bankruptcy, exactly what Gary Smith was predicting.

"Think about it," he said to his uncomfortably quiet audience around the table. "Pretty soon they won't be able to service all that debt. They'll go into default and all their equity will be—"

I finished the sentence with him: "Wiped out."

"That's right," he said. "The stock will go to zero and I'll never have to cover my short."

Hearing Gary's strategy was a seminal event for me. It jived with all of my experiences to that point—the Texas oil bust, Black Monday, my options trading washout, and my growing realization that corporate failure is more prevalent than people like to acknowledge. But I was the only one who appreciated Gary's idea. The rest of our buddies were still giving him confused looks. His strategy was too new for them, too unfamiliar. They couldn't get their minds around it.

A year after that dinner, Prime Motor Inns declared bankruptcy.

FIVE

DECK CHAIRS ON A SINKING SHIP

If the rate of change on the outside exceeds the rate of change on the inside, the end is near.

—Jack Welch

FOR A BRIEF MOMENT IN DECEMBER 2007, I THOUGHT THE video rental chain Blockbuster had hired a movie star to be its director of investor relations. The woman who came out to greet me in the lobby of the company's Dallas headquarters could have easily walked right off the cover of a DVD in one of its stores. She was tall and slender, with silky dark hair and a matinee idol's radiant smile. Her name was Angelika, and her slight eastern European accent made her sound like a femme fatale in a James Bond flick.

"Good morning, Mr. Fearon," she said, extending her hand. "Why don't we speak in my office?"

After I managed to quit stammering, I accepted her offer. You have to understand, I spend almost all of my time meeting with people who look more or less like me—middle-aged guys with boring haircuts in sport coats or oxford shirts. Seeing Angelika that morning was a memorable surprise. Unfortunately for Angelika and everyone else at the company, though, Blockbuster (stock symbol: BBI) was in trouble at the time. It had had three straight money-losing quarters and was on its way to a fourth. It wasn't hard to figure out why. The company was saddled with over nine thousand brick-and-mortar store locations and tens of thousands of employees, at the same time that Netflix—a web-based, ruthlessly efficient competitor with a fraction of its overhead—was pilfering millions of its customers. By the time I flew into Dallas and met with Angelika, the "bust" in the company's name was starting to sound more and more like a foregone conclusion. Its stock price had slid below $4, and it didn't look like it was going to recover.

Despite this bad news, Angelika was upbeat. She enthusiastically predicted a comeback for Blockbuster. I expected her to tell me that the company's managers planned to accomplish this by expanding the online service they had launched to compete with Netflix. But, to my surprise, she said they were actually scaling that effort back.

"We believe our greatest assets are our stores," she stated.

"Your stores? But your stores have been losing money ever since Netflix started."

"That's true, but we plan to use them to generate new revenue streams."

"How?"

"Retail," Angelika announced.

She seemed to think that single word would make me rush out and buy as many shares of BBI as I could find. The frown I was wearing must have informed her that I required a little more convincing, so she cleared her throat and went on.

"We've found that particular products will generate more revenue as sale items rather than rentals," she explained. "Children's movies, for instance. Kids like to watch movies repeatedly, so parents are more inclined to purchase them as opposed to renting them. Video games are also items consumers generally want to own instead of rent."

She presented me with a glossy report detailing the company's plans. "I see," I said with a polite smile as I turned the pages. I was doing my best not to seem rude or dismissive, even though I was highly skeptical.

"We're not just going to sell movies and video games. We plan to offer a whole host of ancillary products as well: movie posters, movie memorabilia, magazines and books about Hollywood. And at the point of purchase, all of our stores will feature theater-style concession items."

"You mean you're going to sell popcorn and Junior Mints, things like that?"

"Yes," Angelika replied happily. She mistook my incredulity for approval. "And we're going to carry the large novelty sizes you can only get in theaters!"

Again, I held my tongue and thanked Angelika for her time. There was no use discussing matters any further. I had heard enough. Angelika escorted me back into the lobby and we exchanged friendly good-byes.

I walked out into the chilly North Texas winter morning with one word playing over and over in my head: *candy*. I just couldn't get past it. Blockbuster's leaders were seriously pitching *candy* sales as the thing that would keep the company from the ash heap. It was almost sad. For a quarter century, Blockbuster had been a massively successful business. Even with all of its recent troubles, it had still had almost $6 billion in revenues the year before my visit. And yet things had gotten so bad so

CAN YOU HEAR ME NOW?

Misguided attempts to preserve an outmoded business model are quite common, and not just at dead companies walking. Starting in the late 2000s, cable television providers began steadily losing subscribers as more and more young consumers in particular "cut the cord" and watched their entertainment online. Big Cable managed to maintain its margins by raising prices. But charging a shrinking pool of customers more for the same product is probably not a sustainable long-term model. In 2013, the cable company in my area briefly pursued what seemed like a Blockbuster-esque strategy: it started aggressively marketing cable-based home phone service. That's right—its salespeople were pushing . . . landline telephones. "Hello, cable providers? Ma Bell called and she wants her business model back." All kidding aside, it's hard to believe that in the age of mobile communication and content delivery that the company's management believed something as old-fashioned as home phones would reverse its slide. Candy sales almost seemed more promising by comparison.

quickly that its executives had been reduced to hoping that selling oversized boxes of Jujyfruits could save it.

Even though I shorted the stocks of three other public video rental chains that wound up going bankrupt, I never shorted Blockbuster. You could say I got "cahned." A few years before my visit with Angelika, renowned investor Carl Icahn had become the biggest shareholder in

Blockbuster and had won a proxy war to control its board of directors. I respected Icahn's acumen, or at least his clout, enough to stay away from shorting Blockbuster while he was so deeply involved. Even if the new retail scheme was as doomed as I thought, I didn't want to be on the wrong side of such a powerful figure. For all I knew, he was prepared to sink a fortune into the company to keep its stock price elevated—and his pockets are a lot deeper than mine.

As it turned out, I completely misread the situation. Icahn wound up being one of the main reasons Blockbuster went broke sooner than later. When he and his allies took over the board in 2005, the CEO at the time was pushing for the company to focus more on the internet. But Icahn got into a feud with him over compensation and eventually brought in a new CEO who implemented the retail strategy.* In other words, Icahn and his handpicked leadership of the company doubled up and tripled up on the very thing that was killing Blockbuster to begin with—the enormous cost burdens of all those locations and employees. Predictably, the company went belly-up as a result. Blockbuster declared bankruptcy in 2010, right after Icahn unloaded all of his shares for pennies on the dollar.

Icahn and his allies at Blockbuster made a classic blunder. Old Wall Street hands call it the buggy whip syndrome: *they failed to recognize that their industry had fundamentally and permanently changed.*

The executives at Cygnus Therapeutics and Shaman Pharmaceuticals, and even Women.com and Quokka Sports, were driven by inspiring ideas. Sure, those companies all failed. But all were developing new,

---

*Aaron Sankin, "How Blockbuster Almost Beat Netflix," *Daily Finance,* November 14, 2014.

innovative products or services. I had a lot of respect for their efforts and even admiration for their passion. I can't say the same for the leadership of Blockbuster. They didn't have the excuse of being caught up in the mania of a captivating story. They were just holding out because they couldn't accept the unpleasant truth that their industry—and the rest of the world—had left them behind.

By the time I got to Dallas, Blockbuster and its storefront model were clearly the horse-drawn carriages of the movie rental business. Netflix and its web-based format were the equivalents of Model A cars. Unlike groceries or prescription pills, consumers liked picking out their DVD rentals online and receiving them in the mail. And they especially liked paying a flat monthly price instead of the exorbitant late fees Blockbuster had been getting fat on for decades. There was no getting around these truths. Netflix already had millions of subscribers in 2007. Just about every other major movie rental chain had already gone broke as a result or was on the brink of it. And yet everyone at Blockbuster did their best to come up with new ways to pretend that things hadn't changed.

At one point, the buzz around the industry was that Blockbuster would save itself by merging with its biggest competitor, Hollywood Video. Here you've got two money-losing companies with identical obsolete business models—and yet somehow, by merging into one giant money-losing company with an obsolete business model, they were magically supposed to become profitable again. When that flawed idea fell through, Blockbuster's brass still did not begin the necessary process of closing stores and investing in their web-based service. Instead, they came up with yet another cockamamie plan to make those stores profitable again, this time by acquiring the nearly bankrupt electronics chain Circuit City. It's hard to believe, but Icahn and the others at Blockbuster seriously thought hawking low-margin gadgets alongside video games and Raisinettes was going to reverse their slide.

The Circuit City deal never happened. But the end was already near. By early 2009, shares of BBI were trading below a buck. A year later, they officially went to zero. Even after the company's bankruptcy, it still took until early 2014 for the last of Blockbuster's stores to close.

The potential mergers of Blockbuster with Hollywood Video and Circuit City were hailed for their potential "operational synergies." Over the years, I have learned to watch out for the word *synergies* when two troubled businesses combine. Recently, it's been bandied about over and over again as money-losing media companies have been consolidating with each other. In 2010, media mogul Barry Diller acquired the moribund *Newsweek* magazine and merged it with an unprofitable news and gossip website called *The Daily Beast,* citing—you guessed it—potential synergies. Three years and millions of dollars in losses later, Diller cried uncle and divested himself of *Newsweek.** I'm not saying mergers can't be beneficial. But all of the synergy in the world cannot replace the lifeblood of any business: growing revenues.

The real tragedy of Blockbuster's history is that it almost escaped its fate. For a little while after Icahn took over, its Total Access online service managed to slow Netflix's momentum. But without late fees and per-movie charges, it was never going to be profitable for the company—not with the burden of thousands of store leases and tens of thousands of employee salaries to pay. But instead of closing as many stores as they could to cut costs and putting everything they could into its online presence,

---

*Leslie Kaufman and Christine Haughney, "The Last Temptation of Tina Brown," *New York Times,* August 4, 2013.

Blockbuster's leadership went backward and decided to turn its stores into glorified candy racks.

I am definitely not trying to bash Carl Icahn. I have a lot of respect for him. But as he has admitted, he blew it big time at Blockbuster. The only way it was going to survive was by adapting to the fact that *people weren't going to get in their cars and drive several miles to a store just so they could overpay to rent movies anymore.* Instead, he wagered that people would continue to drive several miles to overpay for movie rentals if they could also buy candy and magazines and video games—or maybe a cheap flat-screen TV—at the same time.

Compare these desperate attempts to cling to Blockbuster's antiquated business model with the way Netflix, its onetime chief nemesis, has evolved. The entertainment delivery sector is so fast moving, Netflix's DVD-by-mail method was already well on its way to obsolescence before Blockbuster went Chapter 11. Netflix's management recognized this and reacted proactively. Unfortunately, they were almost too aggressive in switching to streaming movies and television shows online. Like JCPenney's leadership, Netflix infamously fired their customers when they suddenly spun off the company's DVD service and jacked up prices. After losing hundreds of thousands of subscribers in a matter of weeks, Netflix quickly reversed this misstep and transitioned to the new platform more gradually, which allowed the company to keep its market share and compete with big new players like Amazon. Netflix also began producing its own original content.

TANKS? WHAT TANKS?

There is a famous story from the invasion of Iraq in 2003. Standing out on the streets of Baghdad, some reporters asked Iraqi information

BLOCKBUSTER REDUX

I've read varying reports on exactly how much money Icahn lost on his Blockbuster investment. Some media outlets put the figure at over $300 million. The *Wall Street Journal* said it was more like $185 million. Either way, there's no doubt that he took a major hit. Icahn himself called it the "worst investment" of his career.

In 2012, Icahn tried to gain control of Netflix. After trying to split its DVD-by-mail business, Blockbuster's once-thriving rival had hit a rough patch. In just fifteen months, Netflix's stock price had tumbled from over $300 to less than $60. That's when Icahn started buying up every share of Netflix he could, professing that he could help turn the company around. Netflix's directors, no doubt remembering the debacle at Blockbuster, quickly passed a "poison pill" stock agreement that raised the cost of shares for anyone who acquired more than 10 percent of the company.

Icahn's reaction to the move reminded me of why I decided not to short Blockbuster: "If they want to go to war, then we'll go to war."*

---

*Greg Bensinger and Anupreeta Das, "Icahn vs. Hastings: The Fight for the Future of Netflix," *Wall Street Journal*, November 14, 2012.

minister Mohammed Said al-Sahaf—better known in the West as Baghdad Bob—if US forces had crossed into the city. Mr. al-Sahaf scoffed and declared, "There are no American troops in Baghdad!" just as a column of M1 Abrams tanks appeared behind him.

When I first heard that story, I couldn't help but think of the executives I've interviewed over the years who have assured me their companies are doing just fine while the walls are almost literally coming down around their ears. If anything, Angelika and the rest of the Blockbuster crew seemed proactive in comparison to some of these folks. At least they tried to do *something* with their retail idea, even if it was misguided. You'd be surprised how rare that kind of initiative is at failing companies whose industries have left them behind. Most of the time, the best people can do in that situation is come up with Baghdad Bob–style denials of reality.

I remember the CFO of another Dallas-based company called Page-Net (stock symbol: PAGE) spending a solid hour trying to convince me that pagers would continue to be a profitable business. This was in 1999, several years before the advent of smartphones but well past the time when it should have been obvious that cell phones were going to make beepers historical relics. And yet to hear this executive talk, pagers were the coolest must-have gizmos of the new millennium. They were more lightweight than portable phones, he told me; they had longer battery life, and they were cheaper.

"Our newest model is the size of a matchbook," he boasted, digging one out of his pocket and presenting it for my inspection. "We see incredible opportunities for expansion in developing markets. Asia, Africa, and Latin America are all prime new areas we intend to pursue aggressively."

"But cellular technology is getting lighter and cheaper, too," I said as I handed the beeper back to him. "Why won't phone companies be able to expand into those markets at the same time as you do?"

The CFO gave me a blank look, then switched to a more scatter-shot technique, peppering me with a series of dubious rationales. Doctors and other busy professionals would always prefer pagers to phones, he claimed. People could send and receive text messages with new two-way pagers. And pagers generally had better penetration in buildings and other indoor spaces than portable phones.

"We understand that many people will likely adopt cellular technology in the coming years," the CFO conceded as our meeting neared a close. "But we're confident that consumers will continue to use pagers so that they can enjoy the added convenience of returning calls on their own time."

Now it was my turn to give him a blank look.

"Are you saying you expect people to carry both a pager *and* a cell phone?"

"Absolutely," the CFO replied with an emphatic nod. I began to get the distinct impression that he was working to convince *himself* of this as much as me. "We have conducted a number of marketing surveys that have shown many people who own both cellular phones and pagers prefer to give out their pager number while keeping their phone number private. That way, they can screen any incoming communications and return only the calls they want to return. Like I said, it is an added convenience."

I suspected at the time that PageNet's CFO was beginning to doubt his own arguments. At least, I hope that's the case. He seemed like a perfectly intelligent, rational person. I'd like to think he could see the gaping holes in what he was saying.

For one thing, how does having to keep track of two different wireless devices count as an added convenience? And he and his colleagues at PageNet couldn't have been unfamiliar with the fact that cell phone companies were already offering text messaging and Caller ID as standard features of nearly every calling plan. Why would someone buy an entirely different device to send texts when they could already do so with their phone? And why would they give out a pager number to screen their calls when they could just look at the readout on their phone and decide which calls to take and which calls to let go to voice mail?

The next morning, I shorted PAGE. For good measure, I also shorted the only other publicly traded paging company still clinging to life at that point. Within two years, they had both gone to zero.

Major secular shifts like the switch to mobile phones and online movie delivery aren't the only ways businesses get left behind. Far more subtle changes in consumer behavior or industry practices can be just as deadly if a company's leaders cling to old strategies and fail to adapt. In 2005, I flew to Denver to visit the headquarters of a chain called Ultimate Electronics (stock symbol: ULTE), which specialized in high-end audio equipment and helpful, knowledgeable staff. Ultimate was a haven for audio and video connoisseurs. By the time I flew in to check it out, it was also on the verge of going broke. It had been able to survive longer than most consumer electronics businesses because it had offered specialty equipment that its competitors couldn't, or wouldn't, stock. But the bigger chains had caught on to Ultimate's game. They'd started to sell that same gear for lower prices. Not surprisingly, in the years prior to my visit, Ultimate's revenues had dropped and its debt levels had mounted.

I sat down with the company's chief financial officer, who had just moved out to Denver from another soon-to-be bankrupt electronics chain in California called The Good Guys. The first thing I asked him was how Ultimate was going to compete with Best Buy, Costco, and the other larger big-box retailers. His answer was about as convincing as the CFO of PageNet, claiming that people would shell out good money for both a pager and a cell phone.

"Our founder started this company so that he could serve people who loved electronics as much as he did," the CFO replied. "He wanted to help them find the best quality brands in the world. It was his passion and it still is. And people still value that kind of expertise and service."

"But these days, Best Buy and Costco have a lot of the same brands that you carry," I countered. "And they're able to sell them for a lot cheaper."

"But they don't offer the knowledge and the personal touch that we do. Our sales teams work with our customers to make sure they get the absolute top equipment on the market. It's right there in our name. We want to give people the ultimate best."

I thanked him and strolled back to my rental car. I didn't need to hear anymore. The next day, I shorted the company's stock. I could see that Ultimate's management was badly misreading the market and refusing to revise their clearly outmoded approach. Just because the founder wanted to help people find good merchandise didn't mean those people were going to pay a premium for that service—not when they could drive down the street and get the same stuff for 10 or 20 percent less!

Put simply, for almost anything more expensive than small luxuries like Starbucks coffee, most Americans shop on one thing and one thing alone: price. This is especially true when you're talking about retailers selling identical products. If you're stocking the same brands as your competitors and they're selling them cheaper than you are, you're dead. You can have the kindest, most solicitous salespeople in the world and you'll still have empty stores. Even affluent people who are willing to pay a lot for top-of-the-line brands like a good bargain. They'll even push a rickety shopping cart through a giant warehouse store to get one.

The guys at Costco figured this out, and that's why they've done so well. But Ultimate's brass refused to face this fact. They wanted to believe that consumers would sacrifice a deal for convenience and for expert help. That was a fatal delusion. The company filed for bankruptcy less than a year after my trip to Denver.

B IS FOR BANKRUPT

The worst Baghdad Bob–esque pitch I've ever heard from an executive clinging to a dying industry came from yet another Dallas-based firm. I already mentioned it in chapter 2, about the dangers of relying too much on formulas. In late 2008, I interviewed the CEO of one of the two remaining publicly traded Yellow Pages companies. His name was Scott, and at that point his company was called Idearc. As I said in that chapter, its headquarters were in the old Braniff Airlines buildings in the middle of Dallas–Fort Worth airport. Floor-to-ceiling windows in Scott's office looked out on airliners as they taxied out for takeoff and screamed down the tarmac.

It was a weird setting for a weird meeting.

Scott was a tall, hard-charging guy with wavy hair and a natural salesman's charismatic smile. We bonded for a moment over the fact that we not only shared the same first name, we'd also both lived in Palo Alto, California, and Evanston, Illinois—I as a student at Stanford and then Northwestern, he in his former job as a venture capitalist. After those pleasantries, Scott proceeded to inform me that Yellow Pages were not only going to survive, they were going to thrive.

"In five years, we'll be making more money than we're making right now," he predicted. "First we're going to cut costs and invest in our new website. Then, once we've got our costs under control, we expect revenues will stabilize and we will return to profitability."

I had checked out the company's website before the meeting, and I had been less than impressed with it. It was little more than a digital copy of the old-fashioned paper version of the Yellow Pages. I couldn't figure out why Scott and his colleagues thought users would go through the extra trouble of logging on to their site, *then* conducting their search for a plumber or a pizza delivery place or whatever else they were looking for. Why wouldn't they cut out the middleman and just use Google or Bing or Yahoo! or any other search engine? When I asked Scott about this, he didn't seem terribly concerned. In fact, he was downright blasé about their transition to the web.

"We expect some adoption of our online services, somewhere in the 10 percent range. But our bread and butter will always be our traditional books."

I had to let that statement sink in. Behind Scott, a big 747 rumbled by on the way to takeoff. Was he seriously saying that he thought consumers would keep hauling out cinderblock-sized publications just to find phone numbers? Remember: this was late 2008, almost two years after the launch of the iPhone.

"If I said the words *Yellow Pages* to my son," I told Scott, "he would think I was talking about a coloring book. Most people under thirty are the same way. So how can you say consumers are going to keep using your printed products? The next generation doesn't even know they exist."

"Your son grew up in Marin, am I right?" Scott countered.

"Yes," I answered. "What does that have to do with anything?"

"Everything. Kids in well-to-do communities grow up around technology. It's second nature to them. But people in the Bay Area aren't like people in the middle of the country. People in places like Kansas and Arkansas and Oklahoma, they still rely on our books. And they're not going to stop. They just do things differently there."

"Are you saying people in the Midwest are too stupid to use a smartphone or to log on to the internet?"

"Not at all. It's a matter of habits and what people are comfortable with, that's all. People trust our brand. It's what their parents used and their grandparents, too. And local merchants know they have to advertise with us if they want to reach the people in their communities."

If you've read the entire book up to this point, you know that I pride myself on, and have made a lot of money by, knowing what most Americans consumers like and don't like. I'm not an expert by any stretch, and I'm not always right, but I think I've shown a knack for it over my career. I knew Americans were never going to get excited about yacht racing, even if they could watch it from dozens of camera angles on the internet. I knew they were never going to buy take-home cholesterol tests or Rollerblades, either. I'm normally the guy telling executives on either coast about how people in the so-called flyover states are likely to behave. So it was surreal to find myself in the opposite position—especially when the guy lecturing me on what Americans preferred was a former venture capitalist.

"Scott," I said with a laugh. "Didn't we just spend ten minutes talking about how you've lived in Palo Alto, California, and Evanston, Illinois, for most of your life? No offense, but what do you know about people in Kansas or Arizona or the Texas Panhandle?"

For the first time in the entire meeting, Scott's smile vanished. We went back and forth for another hour or so as planes continued to taxi by us. Scott really thought he could convince me that people would continue to use the Yellow Pages. After a while, I stuck around for the sheer amusement of watching him continue to try. I only met him that one time, but I can say he was the hardest-working—or at least hardest-*talking*—executive I've ever dealt with. Too bad all that effort was going into a lost cause.

Warren Buffett once said, "When a management with a reputation for brilliance tackles a business with a reputation for poor fundamental economics, it is the reputation of the business that remains intact."* Scott's tenure at Idearc proved this maxim. He was brought in to reverse the company's decline, and for a little while, he managed to improve its EBITDA (earnings before interest, taxes, depreciation, and amortization) figures enough to boost its stock price. But in the end, he couldn't overcome the company's "poor fundamental economics." Less than a year after that meeting near the tarmac of DFW airport, Idearc filed for bankruptcy.

I'd like to make one thing clear, in case I haven't already: I am not sharing these stories to mock or disparage Scott, the CFO of PageNet, Angelika, or anyone else involved in failing businesses. These were not incompetent or dishonest people. They were simply caught up in very bad situations. They made good faith efforts to deal with those situations, but like so many before them and many more to come, they did not succeed. There is no shame in that.

When it comes to pagers or the Yellow Pages, there really wasn't much else the people at Idearc or PageNet could have done to stave off the inevitable. The march of progress hadn't just left those industries behind, it had trampled them underfoot. Blockbuster, on the other hand, probably could have saved itself. But it would have taken a radical, and very

---

*Warren Buffett, Chairman's Letter, *Berkshire Hathaway Annual Report,* 1980.

painful, restructuring to do so. Understandably, not many executives are willing to close thousands of their stores and lay off tens of thousands of their employees, even if that is the only way to keep a company in business. So, like the brass at Blockbuster, most choose more hopeful, less draconian tactics. But in my experience, half measures almost always hasten rather than delay the end.

To be honest, I've only seen one person in my three decades of managing money who was willing—even eager—to remake a company whose industry had left it behind. It was during my time at Texas Commerce Bank, way back in the sticky Houston summer of 1984. I was primarily in charge of analyzing energy stocks like Global Marine for the bank's trust accounts. But I was also responsible for keeping track of companies in the consumer services sector, which included hotels, motels, restaurants, and—most important for me, as it turned out—airlines.

At the time, there was an airline company headquartered in Houston called Texas Air. Its CEO was a fiery native New Yorker named Frank Lorenzo. In 1981, after a grueling takeover bid, he and Texas Air had acquired Continental Airlines, which wound up declaring bankruptcy in the fall of 1983. Continental was still in business as Texas Air's prime operating subsidiary, but it was only serving a fraction of the routes it had once served. Because of these troubles, shares of Texas Air were very cheap, down around $5. And yet, when I crunched the numbers and plotted out the company's earnings models, I found something intriguing: of all the airlines in business, Texas Air had the lowest "cost per available seat-mile," meaning it could charge less for tickets and still make a healthy profit.

I checked and rechecked my calculations to make sure they were correct. When I was satisfied that I hadn't made a stupid error, I started to go into my boss Geoff Raymond's office to show him what I had found. But then I figured it was time I tried to fly this one solo, so I sat back down at my desk and looked up the phone number for Texas Air's offices. A receptionist answered my call and informed me that the company's director of investor relations was not available, but that he would return my call soon. I thought I might hear back the next day, or maybe sometime the following week. It was around lunchtime so I went downstairs and bought a sandwich at a shop called Antoine's across the street. Less than an hour later, as I was eating the second half of that sandwich at my desk, my phone rang. I answered it with my mouth half full. A fast-talking man with a thick Queens accent said he was looking for Scott Fearon.

"You've found him," I replied, swallowing the rest of my food. "How can I help you?"

"This is Frank Lorenzo. I heard you were interested in talking about my company."

I sat up in my chair and frantically tried to dig my file on Texas Air out from beneath my lunch. The only thing I succeeded at doing was dropping the rest of my sandwich on the floor. You have to understand, I had just turned twenty-five years old. I was barely one year out of business school. Frank Lorenzo was, and still is, a legend in the corporate world, and here he was speaking into my ear.

"Yes, Mr. Lorenzo," I managed to say. "I would very much like to discuss Texas Air with you, but I know you must be a very busy man so I—"

"I'm about to go for a run," he cut in. "Can you be here in two hours?"

"Yes, sir," I croaked. "I'll be there."

THE F***ING HAM IN THE
F***ING HAM SANDWICH

Lorenzo's office was on the twenty-eighth floor of the American General Tower, a sand-colored high-rise a few miles west of downtown on Allen Parkway. He was studying some paperwork behind his desk when I came in. Even though he'd just come back from what I later found out was a daily ten-mile jog in the sweltering midday heat, there wasn't a drop of sweat on his brow. His dark hair was parted neatly to one side and a bespoke Italian suit hung loosely on his wiry frame. There's no other way to put it: the man was imposing. Leaning back in his leather chair with the skyline of Houston spread out behind him, he looked like the perfect embodiment of the 1980s corporate raider—which, in many ways, he was. A few years after our meeting, he waged a storied takeover battle for Eastern Airlines with none other than Carl Icahn.

Several scale models of DC-10s were displayed around his office. One of these was painted in Continental's colors, another had the now-defunct Texas International Air brand on the side of it, and a third had been decorated with the name and logo of Jet Capital, the holding company Lorenzo and a fellow Harvard MBA had started in the late 1960s. I'd done a little research on him in the two hours between our phone call and our meeting, and I'd learned that his nickname at Harvard had been "Frankie Smooth Talk." He definitely lived up to that nickname in our meeting—at least the "talk" part. I'm not sure a man who used profanity like most people use nouns could be called smooth, though.

When I brought up Continental's bankruptcy, Lorenzo got particularly, well, *frank.*

"I'll tell you a little secret, Mr. Fearon," he said. "We didn't have to take Continental chapter when we did. We could have limped along for a while longer. But I said screw it, we're going to have to do this at some point, so we might as well do it on our terms. The sooner the better."

"You mean, you *chose* to go bankrupt?" I asked. I couldn't mask my surprise. This was a very odd concept back in the early 1980s, especially for a young kid like me. In business school, people talked about bankruptcy a lot like you would expect them to talk about getting arrested for drunk driving. It was something shameful.

"Hell yes, I chose to go bankrupt!" Lorenzo almost shouted. "There was no other way to do what had to be done." He leaned forward and put both elbows on his desk. "Here's the thing. Before we went Chapter 11, Continental was the f***ing ham in the f***ing ham sandwich."

"Excuse me?"

Lorenzo laid one hand on top of another. "Here's a sandwich, okay? Only it's not a sandwich. It's the airline industry. The top slice of bread is the legacy carriers, American, United, Pan Am, those guys. Now, everybody knows their prices are outrageous. They're way, way overpriced because they've got high labor costs. But they get away with it because business travelers use them. They're flying on a corporate expense account, so they don't give a damn what a ticket costs. They just want legroom and a decent meal and some good-looking stewardesses who smile and say nice things to them, right?"

He paused and waited for me to show that I was still listening, which I was—very intently. Being in Lorenzo's company was like attending a weird cross between a Vegas variety show and a graduate seminar in high finance. I didn't know whether to laugh out loud or take notes, so I just sat there perfectly still and tried my best to keep up.

"Right," I said.

"Now," he continued while shaking the hand on the bottom. "Down here on the bottom of the sandwich, you've got this new low-fare company called Southwest. They don't care about frills. They sell you a cheap ticket and they say, 'Here, have some peanuts, pal, we'll be landing in an hour, the barf bag is in the seat pocket in front of you if you need it.' Let me tell you something, Mr. Fearon. Those guys at Southwest are kicking everybody's butts. They're completely changing this industry. These guys on top here, American and United and all the other legacy companies? They're in trouble, they just don't know it yet. But in a couple years, they're going to be in the same place Continental was."

Again he paused to let me demonstrate that I was still with him.

"You mean, they're going to be the ham in the sandwich?" I offered.

"Exactly!" Lorenzo cried as he rubbed his hands together. "Continental was right in the middle. We had the high labor costs of the legacy guys, but we didn't offer the same level of service, so business travelers wouldn't fly with us. But because we had all those labor costs, we had to charge too much to compete with Southwest. So there you go. We were the ham in the sandwich. We were dead meat, unless we did something. So we did. It wasn't pleasant. A lot of people lost their jobs or took pay cuts. But it worked."

"It did?" I asked.

"Hell yes! You saw our cost per seat-mile number. It's incredible! The bankruptcy allowed us to renegotiate all of our labor contracts. We cut our least profitable routes, too. Let me tell you something, we're back. Our turnaround is going to shock the world."

He clapped his hands together triumphantly and sat back contentedly in his chair. I half-expected him to light up a celebratory cigar.

That afternoon, I drove back to my office at Texas Commerce Bank and typed up a two-page summary of my research, including a brief description of my meeting with Frank "Smooth Talk" Lorenzo. I paraphrased his more colorful language and concluded by saying that I thought we should invest heavily in Texas Air. It was my first "strong buy" recommendation at the bank. I hardly slept that night. I was too excited to find out if the higher-ups would follow my advice. The next morning, Geoff Raymond gave me the green light to purchase a million shares, which I did right after leaving his office.

There's nothing quite like spending $5 million of other people's money before your second cup of coffee.

As I said, because of Continental's bankruptcy, Texas Air's stock price had taken a major hit. It was down to $5 when we bought in. The rest of Wall Street had pretty much written the company off for dead. Then its quarterly earnings report came out, and—true to Lorenzo's pre-diction—it freaked people out. Continental was not only still alive, it was suddenly making money, a lot of money. With cheaper labor contracts in place, every ticket it sold was highly profitable. And thanks to newly discounted fares, it was selling out most of its flights.

A few days after the company announced its record-level quarterly earnings, Texas Air's stock had already doubled. Then it doubled again, and again, and kept going up. By the time I left TCB for GT Capital in San Francisco three years later, it was up around fifty bucks, a full ten times what we had paid for it. It wouldn't be an exaggeration to say that investment made the early part of my career. It was one of the biggest winners of my time at Texas Commerce. And given the path I've chosen since then, it seems fitting that my best-performing investment during my four years in Houston owed its success to bankruptcy.

SHOCK THERAPY

Frank Lorenzo, as many of you may know, is a very controversial figure. If you ever drop his name to a longtime union member in the airline industry, I suggest you duck, or at least cover your ears. The reaction is bound to be forceful, and not very pleasant. I am certainly not trying to make Lorenzo out to be a saint here. As a matter of fact, after Texas Commerce's big investment in Texas Air came out, I was interviewed by a reporter at the *Wall Street Journal,* and I said that I was worried that Lorenzo seemed to care more about financial wheeling and dealing than the day-to-day work of managing an airline. The next morning, that quote appeared on the front page of the paper, and I found myself summoned from my cubicle on the fourth floor of the Texas Commerce Tower way up to the sixty-eighth story. Several executives there warned me, with Lorenzo-like frankness, that if I ever spoke to the press again, I would be riding the elevator to the ground floor one last time.

Even though it was stupid of me to talk to a reporter about my concerns, what I said was from the heart. Lorenzo did worry me. I knew he was a brilliant businessman, and his use of bankruptcy as a tool to remake Continental was unprecedented. It was creative destruction in its rawest, most potent form. But in the end, everything just seemed like a game of numbers to him. In fact, the second time I came to see him a few months after our first meeting, he offered me a job analyzing potential takeover targets for Jet Capital and Texas Air. That was plainly where his focus was—making deals and growing his assets, not managing the companies he already owned.

Lorenzo's ruthless form of capitalism had its advantages, but it was incredibly risky. Taking Continental into bankruptcy was a kind of

NOSEDIVE

My experience with Texas Air notwithstanding, the airline industry has historically been one of the worst sectors to invest in. The costs of running an airline are astronomical, and cutthroat competition constantly puts downward pressure on prices (and profits). High costs and poor margins: that's not exactly a lucrative business model. It almost makes the restaurant industry look like a gold mine by comparison. And yet—just like in the restaurant business—one high-profile figure after another, from Donald Trump to Carl Icahn, has poured millions into their own pet airline ventures. In almost every case, these investments have crashed and burned.

Warren Buffett has repeatedly lamented the vast amounts of money airline investors—whom he once jokingly referred to as "aeroholics"—have lost over the decades. "If a capitalist had been present at Kittyhawk back in the early 1900s," he told the *Telegraph* newspaper, "he should have shot Orville Wright. He would have saved his progeny a lot of money."*

---

*Dominic Lawson, Robert Peston, and Grant Ringshaw, "Buffett: My Elephant Gun Is Loaded," *Telegraph,* September 22, 2002.

corporate shock therapy. In that particular case, the patient lived through the procedure and regained its health. But a few years later, he tried to apply the same technique at Eastern Airlines; this time, the patient died on the operating table. The company imploded and never reemerged from bankruptcy. And Continental itself suffered in the long term under Lorenzo's leadership. By 1990, shortly after he sold off his stake, it was back in bankruptcy.

For all my reservations about his motives, I have no doubt that Lorenzo made the right decision with Continental in 1983. As he himself pointed out, Southwest had permanently changed the airline business with its discount model. There was no getting around that. Lorenzo knew that Continental had to reinvent itself to stay alive. His methods were drastic. But they were necessary. And just as he predicted that summer afternoon in his office, the other legacy carriers have been forced to adopt them. In the thirty years since Lorenzo willingly took Continental into bankruptcy, every single major US airline except Southwest has filed for bankruptcy at least once. Some, like Continental and United, have even filed multiple times.

SIX

THE BUCK STOPS . . . THERE

Victory has a thousand fathers, but defeat is an orphan.

—John F. Kennedy

What, me worry?

—Alfred E. Neuman

IN THE SUMMER OF 2007, I VISITED THE NICEST CORPO-
rate office I've ever been in. Unfortunately, it belonged to the president
and CEO of a business fast on its way to bankruptcy.

His name was Rob, and he had a beautifully appointed corner aerie
on the thirty-second floor of Embarcadero Center Four in the Financial District of San Francisco. His company, Building Materials Holding
Corporation (stock symbol: BMHC), sold construction materials and
services to housing developers. It had originally been owned by the old
Boise Cascade lumber company in Idaho, but it had moved west to its
fancy new digs after a massive acquisition spree in the 1990s had turned

it into a billion-dollar concern. I had actually met Rob once before, in 2002, but when he escorted me into his office overlooking San Francisco Bay that second time, the view almost knocked me flat. Unlike my previous visit, and on most summer days in the city, the fog had miraculously held off, and it seemed like it was clear enough to see all the way over the golden brown hills of Marin County to the Oregon border. The bay far below us was as blue as sapphire and as smooth as a sateen bed sheet. Across busy Embarcadero Boulevard, boats the size of toys landed and took off from the Ferry Building. To my right, a container ship eased beneath the silver arch of the Bay Bridge. To my left, the Golden Gate Bridge glowed orange in the late afternoon sunlight.

"How do you like the scenery?" Rob asked in a deadpan as I stared out the floor-to-ceiling windows.

He let me gawk for a little while longer before he invited me to sit down. His office was large enough to include a polished mahogany conference table in one corner. I fumbled with my notes at first. The gorgeous vista almost made me forget the point of my visit, which was to discuss BMHC's extremely ugly finances.

At the time, the housing market was just starting to transition from a temporary correction to an epic meltdown, and Building Materials Holding Corporation was starting to look like a major reclamation project because of it. After producing record profits in 2006 at the peak of the boom, its business had eroded faster than Alan Greenspan's reputation. Year over year, the number of building permits taken out for single-family homes had dropped roughly 30 percent, and BMHC's profits were falling more than twice as fast. Its net income for the first six months of 2007 was roughly $14.5 million. On paper, that's not a terrible number, until you compared it to the $62 million the company made in the same period the previous year. Not surprisingly, BMHC's debts were growing almost as fast as its earnings were dropping. It had always carried a good deal of debt in order to finance its acquisitions, but in those same first six months of 2007, it had taken on an additional $84 million in liabilities, and its total long-term debt stood at a troubling $435.5 million.

Not many businesses can weather such a swift reversal in their core market without making painful reductions in operating expenses, and BMHC was cutting back somewhat. Rob told me the company had laid off a good number of employees and was closing some of its regional offices. He also delivered a standard speech about the cyclical nature of the housing market and how he and most experts believed that it was near its bottom. At the time, I wasn't fully aware of just how gruesome the crash was going to be (this was more than a year before I visited the doomed Brightwater development in Orange County). For all I knew, Rob was right and the downturn was going to be relatively short-lived. But sitting in his opulent, top-floor office in some of the most expensive commercial real estate in the country—if not the world—I couldn't help but sense a troubling disconnect between Rob's reassuring words and reality. There was also the matter of his suit. Rob had the dapper style and quietly confident air of a top-notch lawyer, which is exactly what he was before taking the reins of BMHC. I don't know men's fashion well enough to guess the exact brand of his beautifully tailored three-piece or how much it cost, but I'm sure that it was a good deal more expensive than most people's monthly mortgage payments.

I'm not knocking Rob for his good taste in clothing or offices. But neither his suit nor his work environment, not to mention his bullish demeanor, gave me the sense that he had a clear view of the disaster his company was facing. As I went over BMHC's horrendous financial statements with him, I remembered the old story of Emperor Nero practicing his fiddle while Rome burned. Rob clearly wasn't as incompetent, or depraved, as Nero. He'd helmed BMHC for a decade by then; under his leadership, it had grown from a regional outfit to the sixth-largest lumber and building materials company in the country. But it had done so by following the dangerous formula of hypergrowth. Rob and his predecessor as CEO had boosted the company's balance sheets (and stock price) by taking on debt to buy out dozens of smaller competitors. The formula worked well during boom times, when BMHC could service that debt with growing profits. But as soon as things turned and revenues declined, all that leverage suddenly teetered over the company like one of the towering Northwest conifers Boise Cascade felled by the thousands during its heyday.

Making matters worse, BMHC was still primarily a commodity-driven business. It might have been easy for Rob and its other executives to forget, on the thirty-second floor of one of San Francisco's most exclusive business addresses, but the firm made its money framing up suburban tract homes and wholesaling low-margin commodities like plywood, drywall, and roof shingles. That is a brutal, highly volatile industry. One two-by-four or bag of concrete is identical to another, and developers aren't going to pay more for them just because they like you or you wear an impressive suit. For BMHC, like every other commodity business, the only way to compete is on price. That's hard enough to do, but it's downright impossible when you're carrying exorbitant administrative expenses—like, say, hundred-dollar-a-square-foot waterfront office space—or you're paying your top executives enough to dress like they just stepped off a runway in Milan. Rob's total annual compensation was reportedly well into seven figures.

I wasn't the only person in the investing world concerned about the gulf between BMHC's rapidly declining finances and its leadership's lofty lifestyle. Just a few months before I visited Embarcadero Center, a money manager in Los Angeles named Robert Chapman had taken advantage of BMHC's plummeting stock price to acquire more than 7 percent of the company. Chapman has never been shy about criticizing the managers of businesses he invests in, but he was particularly pointed with the brass at BMHC. He took to publicly calling out Rob as "San Francisco's own $6 Million Man" and urged the company to reduce "its bloated cost structure."[*]

Even as the housing crisis became a clear supercycle event, BMHC—again, a low-margin commodity and service provider with its roots in Boise, Idaho—kept its tony corporate headquarters on the San Francisco waterfront. That fact alone, even more than the firm's increasingly gruesome finances, convinced me to short its stock. Relatively speaking, the expense of maintaining the San Francisco office might have been small compared to BMHC's overall budget, but the symbolism of it was enormous. It displayed a leadership that was, quite literally, out of touch. Responsible managers would have already moved themselves into much humbler surroundings. There was no reason Rob and his fellow executives couldn't conduct their business in a low-cost industrial park or even some modest mobile offices tucked into the corner of one of the dozens of lumber supply yards the company owned. That would have not only saved crucial overhead expenses during the housing crisis, it would have shown the world—and their own employees—that they were going to do

[*]Chapman Capital LLC, Schedule 13d filing for Building Materials Holding Corporation, June 5, 2007.

everything it took to weather the downturn, even if it meant living and working (gasp!) outside of San Francisco.

Eventually, in early 2009, BMHC did move its headquarters back to its original hometown of Boise, Idaho. But by then, it was too late to save the business. The New York Stock Exchange had already delisted its stock. Six short months later, BMHC filed for bankruptcy and its stock went to zero. The company emerged from Chapter 11 in much better shape as a private concern. Not surprisingly, Rob did not make it through the reorganization. He stepped down as CEO and was replaced by someone making a fraction of his salary. I haven't been to visit this new CEO's office in Boise. I'm sure it's not quite as impressive as Rob's old suite in Embarcadero Center. Then again, I've been to Idaho and it has plenty of breathtaking scenery, too.

THE EMPEROR WEARS NO CLOTHES
(AND DOESN'T SELL ANY EITHER)

A euphemism that gets thrown around a lot in the corporate world is *disruption*. New technologies or services are said to disrupt existing industries, forcing businesses to adapt or perish. While many people act like this is a new phenomenon birthed in a garage in Silicon Valley, it's actually a very old process. Almost every business faces some kind of disruptive event in its lifetime, and it's up to its managers to make sure that it evolves and continues to compete. But when those managers don't disrupt their own lifestyles to bring the changes about, their efforts are almost always doomed. It's like trying to lead a cavalry charge from behind. If you're not willing to take a bullet yourself, you're not going to inspire many people to follow you into battle.

Several years after my experience with BMHC, the board of the department store giant JCPenney handpicked another affluent Bay Area executive, Ron Johnson, to be its CEO. The hire was hailed by Wall Street and the media, and JCPenney's stock shot up five points on the day of the announcement. At that point, Johnson was the darling of the business world. He had built Apple's retail stores into a juggernaut, and people were understandably optimistic that he could revamp the old department store chain as well. But I remember hearing something at the time that kept me from sharing in this positive outlook: when he took the job, Johnson refused to move near the company's headquarters in Plano, Texas. Instead, he kept his house in a high-rent Silicon Valley suburb. Later it was revealed that he flew the three-thousand-mile round-trip each week on the company's private jet and stayed at the exclusive Dallas Ritz-Carlton on JCPenney's tab.

As I mentioned in chapter 3, a few months after Johnson's firing, I visited JCPenney's Plano headquarters and spoke with a top executive. He pointed out the window toward a perfectly decent midrange hotel across the freeway from the campus. He said he could have reserved the nicest suite they had for Johnson at that establishment. For the money it cost the company to put Johnson up at the Ritz-Carlton, he probably could have rented out an entire floor.

As with Rob at BMHC, Johnson's decision to keep his residence in the Bay Area and stay at the Ritz was largely symbolic. At the time of his hiring, JCPenney had over $17.7 billion in annual revenues, and in this day and age, it's technologically feasible for a top executive to commute halfway across the country. For those reasons, many JCPenney bulls dismissed Johnson's refusal to move to Plano as insignificant. But his imperial attitude reminded me of Rob, who was running what amounted to a lumber company from the Financial District of San Francisco. That sort of elitism rarely sits well with workers, middle management, or even other executives, and it almost always leads to internal problems. In Johnson's case, it was also a harbinger of something else, which I discussed in chapter 3: his utter cluelessness when it came to the chain's working-class customer base. While that is what ultimately led to his firing, his self-imposed distance from his own workers might have been just as corrosive. You can't make major changes in a company with thousands of employees unless you

BIG BROTHER

Johnson didn't help his elitist image when he reportedly started sending out monthly video addresses (many of them taped from his living room in California) and requiring JCPenney employees to watch them.* That wasn't just imperial, it was downright Orwellian.

Can you imagine being a busy department manager at a store in Lawrence, Kansas, or Columbus, Ohio, and having to take an hour of your day to watch a video of some millionaire in Silicon Valley who purports to care about your company but can't even be bothered to live in the same town as its corporate headquarters? I can't either, and that's why I wasn't surprised to see Johnson's grand experiment at JCPenney fail spectacularly. I even made a little bit of money shorting the company's stock as it fell.

*Kim Bhasin, "Ron Johnson's Desperate Broadcasts to JC Penney Workers Fell Flat as Company Faltered," *Huffington Post*, May 28, 2013.

connect with them directly and earn their loyalty. That's all but impossible when you're literally looking down on them from thirty thousand feet.

Johnson was relieved of his duties at JCPenney a short eighteen months after he took the job. Despite his brief tenure, he managed to bring the century-old retailer to the brink of bankruptcy. In a single year, the company lost well over $1 billion.

As hard as I've been on Rob at Building Materials Holding Corporation and Ron Johnson at JCPenney, you might find it surprising that I don't blame them primarily for their companies' failures. They might have been aloof, but they weren't dishonest or immoral. In fact, they were perfectly upfront about their plans and their priorities—which is why it was shocking that they were hired to begin with, or left in place as long as they were. Then again, the very boards of directors who brought them on were clearly just as out of touch with their businesses as they were. A famous New York hedge fund manager named Bill Ackman, who had a major stake in JCPenney, was responsible for Johnson's hiring. He, like Johnson, wanted to remake JCPenney into a place where coastal elites like him could feel comfortable shopping, despite the fact that most of the thousand-plus stores were in working-class areas in the middle of the country.

Like Rob managing a lumber supply company from the rarified air of San Francisco's Financial District, JCPenney's directors failed to venture beyond their own insulated perspectives when they hired Johnson. Instead of finding someone who understood the company's core customers and business model, they turned the company over to someone exactly like them. That shortsighted nepotism nearly bankrupted one of the largest and most storied retailers in the country's history.

JCPenney was far from the first company to go south because its directors chose an absentee chief executive with no grasp of a business's culture or customers. I've seen this phenomenon a number of times over the years, and it almost always ends badly—not just for the companies, but often for the directors and executives themselves. One of the most infamous examples took place back in the late 1980s when the San Francisco investment bank Hambrecht & Quist—which specialized in rehabbing troubled tech companies—acquired a major stake in a struggling disk drive manufacturer called MiniScribe.

A few years earlier, IBM had dropped MiniScribe disk drives from its PCs, almost killing the company. But Bill Hambrecht, a revered figure in the investment world, believed it could come back. He convinced his fellow directors on MiniScribe's board to hire his personal corporate "Dr. Fix-It," a man named Q. T. Wiles, to make it happen. Wiles had previously turned around several other Hambrecht & Quist investments. But MiniScribe was a different kettle of digital fish. For one thing, it was larger than any of the other companies Wiles had managed. It was also headquartered in Longmont, Colorado, a suburban community about as far away from Denver as Plano is from Dallas. Wiles didn't want to leave his home in the Los Angeles area, so, like Ron Johnson, he tried to run the business from afar. He reportedly traveled to Longmont once a quarter or less. But even though he wasn't physically in their offices, his intense leadership style created so much pressure on MiniScribe's executives that they began to falsify their accounting records to meet his aggressive revenue goals. At one point, they became so desperate to boost their sales figures, they began to ship packages full of bricks instead of disk drives!*

---

*Patrice Apodaca, "Why 'Dr. Fix-It' of High-Tech Firms Failed to Save MiniScribe," *Los Angeles Times,* September 26, 1989.

These frauds went undetected long enough for MiniScribe's finances—and its stock price—to recover briefly. Wiles was credited for rescuing another faltering business. The celebratory champagne went flat fast, though. After the company announced big losses, MiniScribe's creditors and shareholders sued over its cooked books. They also sued Hambrecht & Quist and both Bill Hambrecht and Q. T. Wiles personally. A civil jury eventually awarded the plaintiffs $550 million. Hambrecht & Quist, once one of the most powerful investment firms in the country, almost went bankrupt as a result. Bill Hambrecht's reputation was tarnished, but he got off relatively easy compared to his old friend Q. T. Wiles. In 1994, Wiles was found guilty of fraud and insider trading.*

THE BLAME GAME

Corporate leaders don't have to live thousands of miles from their jobs to be woefully out of touch with the fortunes of their own companies. I've seen lots of committed, hands-on executives make the same mistake but for a different reason. They haven't been as aloof as Ron Johnson or Rob at BMHC, but they've been just as unwilling to admit their own shortcomings. During hard times, they've pointed to all sorts of reasons for their business's troubles when they really should have turned their fingers on themselves.

I am intimately familiar with this tendency to deflect responsibility. While my first restaurant was losing thousands of dollars a week, I identified all sorts of culprits for its troubles—my unreliable staff, the cost of

*Patrice Apodaca, "Sherman Oaks Businessman Found Guilty of Fraud," *Los Angeles Times,* August 9, 1994.

food, the fickle habits of my customers—instead of recognizing the root of the problem from the very beginning: my insistence on serving Cajun food in an area that would never warm to that cuisine.

People don't like to face bad news, especially when it means admitting that they've made stupid decisions. They invent all kinds of rationalizations to keep from owning up to their culpability. Worst of all, they tend to blame anything and everyone but themselves for their failures. The Bible says, "Pride goeth before destruction." I think they should put that quote in business textbooks, because pride often goeth before bankruptcy, too. If you're not willing to admit your own mistakes and misjudgments, you're going to eat them for lunch.

Back in 1991, the first year I started my hedge fund (and right around the time Bill Hambrecht and Q. T. Wiles were in court dealing with the MiniScribe debacle), I paid a visit to a tech company in San Jose called Consilium (stock symbol: CSIM). Consilium built a software product that controlled automated factory operations—the robots that soldered components to computer motherboards and painted new cars on assembly lines, things like that. I'd been studying the numbers and noticed that its debt levels were getting dangerously high at the same time as its revenues were flattening out, so I got in my car and tooled down the peninsula to its headquarters. I met the company's chief financial officer, Mark, who had a ready answer for Consilium's troubles.

"It's very simple, Scott," he said. "It's all about M-1."

"M-1?" I asked. "What do you mean, M-1?"

"M-1," Mark repeated. "The aggregated monetary supply. The Federal Reserve has been constraining it over the last two quarters so factories aren't spending like they used to. That's why sales have been flat."

"Hold on," I said. "M-1 is literally trillions of dollars. You guys do like ten million a quarter in sales. You don't think your problems might have something to do with the quality of your products or what your competitors are doing?"

"Oh no, absolutely not, Scott," he said. "We're rock solid. It's the Fed. I'm telling you. They're killing our business."

I shook his hand, drove back to my office, and immediately shorted Consilium's stock. It was trading at $17 at the time. Over the next year, the company's revenue growth continued to disappoint and its share price turned south. I covered my position at just under $10, but the stock continued to trend down after I got out. In 1998, technology giant Applied Materials acquired Consilium for about $7 a share.

As soon as Mark started spouting off about M-1, I knew Consilium was in trouble. It was obvious that he was looking for any excuse he could find for their problems instead of facing up to the simplest, most obvious explanation: they were selling an inferior product. Like so many other people I've seen in failing businesses, Mark kept casting around for something on the outside to blame when he should have seen where the real problem was—right there inside his own shop.

Sure, macro events like M-1 can affect a business, especially a large business like Oracle or Microsoft or Ford Motor Company. My first employer, Texas Commerce Bank, was one of the most profitable banks in the country before the price of oil collapsed. That massive reversal crippled the company, and scores of others. But the idea that some small variation in the country's multitrillion-dollar money supply would significantly swing the fortunes of a pipsqueak tech firm with a couple million in revenues was laughable. This was reinforced by the fact that, despite Mark's reasoning, Consilium's main competitors were doing fine at the time. Their sales and revenues hadn't been affected by the far-off decisions of central bankers in Washington. And yet, I still remember the look in Mark's eyes as he told me about it. He wasn't lying or spinning some tale for me. He really believed what he was saying.

Big companies play the blame game as much as smaller firms like Consilium. In 2013, tech behemoth Cisco blamed a sizable dip in its offshore sales on revelations that several Silicon Valley companies had helped the US government spy on foreign governments and companies.* This excuse would have seemed a whole lot more plausible if Cisco's main Chinese competitor, a company called Huawei, hadn't been eating into its overseas market share long before news of the spying scandal broke.

Just about every industry has its pet excuse for bad results. Companies in the apparel sector routinely blame the weather for any dip in sales. Winter-focused clothing companies will bemoan unseasonably warm weather while sporting and outdoor clothing companies will cite cold snaps for disappointing results. I remember studying the numbers of one discount retailer in San Antonio called 50-Off Stores and finding the same weather excuse in its financial filings for two straight years. Its managers didn't just blame the weather for the company's poor performance, they used *the exact same wording to do so.* That was a red flag for me, and after crunching the numbers a bit more, I shorted its stock. The repetition of the wording showed me that 50-Off's management team wasn't just refusing to take responsibility for its internal problems, they were too lazy to come up with a new scapegoat. Within a few years, 50-Off was 100 percent bankrupt.

---

*Eamon Javers, "Is Snowden Effect Stalking US Telecom Sales?," CNBC, November 15, 2013.

Another excuse I see is our country's "sluggish economy." That precise phrase is frequently employed in press releases and corporate disclosures. Having lived through a number of genuine economic collapses in my career—the 1980s Texas oil bust, the bursting of the dotcom bubble, and the 2008 financial crisis—I usually find this explanation for disappointing results less than convincing. The US churns out more than $17 *trillion* in economic output every year. We have the most dynamic and sophisticated economy in the history of the world. Blaming an individual company's lackluster performance on slight variations in that ocean-sized system is like saying a typhoon in Japan caused

GROUNDED

The unluckiest dead company walking I've ever shorted was Minnesota-based Wilsons Leather (stock symbol: WLSN). Unlike Consilium, 50-Off Stores, and so many other troubled companies I've encountered, it had every right to blame external events for its failure.

For most of its long history, Wilsons was a profitable, well-managed concern. Shortly before the terrorist attacks of September 11, 2001, it acquired dozens of airport kiosks selling leather luggage and other travel gear. It wasn't a bad business move, unless you count the horrendous timing, which no one could have foreseen. After several months of virtually no air travel following the attacks, and no revenues coming in from the kiosks, Wilsons had no choice but to file for bankruptcy.

flooding in Mazatlán. Sure, it's remotely possible, but there are a whole lot of other factors at play, and what's happening inside a company almost always trumps what's going on outside of it. Also, if you study our GDP numbers, growth in the United States has been consistently sluggish for a long while. And yet plenty of companies have done just fine. In fact, whenever I see the "sluggish economy" chestnut in a disappointing earnings report, I make sure to check how the company's competitors are faring. More often than not, they aren't doing very sluggishly at all.

LONG AND WRONG

As it turned out, Consilium's CFO wasn't the only one refusing to see the writing on the wall when it came to his company's problems. A few months after that meeting in San Jose, I was in the buffet line at the American Electronics Association Conference and got an earful from someone else who thought Consilium was bound to recover. They used to hold the conference at the Hyatt in Monterey every year back then. I was scooping mashed potatoes onto my plate and looking out at the beautiful view of the Pacific when a brash money manager shouldered his way through the crowd and started giving me all kinds of grief for shorting Consilium.

"I've done hundreds of hours of research on that company," he said. "The CEO is a top engineer in Silicon Valley. Consilium is going up, and if you stay short, you're going to lose big. I promise you."

I was more than a little worried that this guy might be right. I only had three million bucks in my hedge fund at that point, and a good chunk of that belonged to me and members of my family. I couldn't afford to be wrong. But I stood my ground and I told him I was going to stick with my decision. Then I went back to my food.

"We'll see," he said ominously. "We'll just see."

We did see, of course. Despite his confidence and his "hundreds of hours" of research, that money manager was wrong. Looking back, the fundamentals of Consilium were obviously flawed. They were a troubled business in a very dynamic, fast-changing sector. And yet I was one of the only people in the investment game to see it. I'm pretty sure the reason for that was the same reason the company's CFO was content to blame M-1: people cannot face their own bad decisions, in business or in investing. The guy who chewed me out in the buffet line wasn't the only money manager who was "long and wrong" in Consilium. Practically everyone misread the company. But no one could bring themselves to reverse course. They forgot that cardinal rule: it's okay to be wrong; it's not okay to *stay* wrong.

Even sophisticated, accomplished investors often hold on to money-losing stocks long past when they should have cut their losses. Many of them even double up and triple up on their stakes by averaging down as stocks fall. They justify these actions by convincing themselves—like Mark at Consilium or Rob at Building Materials Holding Corporation—that external rather than internal factors are causing the companies to struggle. In 2013, I shorted a troubled company called Dendreon (stock symbol: DNDN). The firm produces one of only three viable nonsurgical prostate cancer treatments on the market. Its drug, Provenge, was the first of the three treatments to receive approval from the FDA back in 2010. Dendreon's stock shot up close to $50 on the news, as excited analysts predicted billions in future revenues from the drug. As it turned out, though, the competing treatments—which gained approval shortly after

Provenge—were not only comparably effective but much less expensive to administer. Not surprisingly, they vastly outsold Provenge. Making matters worse, when the company was riding high, Dendreon issued over $600 million in bonds to expand its manufacturing and marketing capabilities. By 2013, its earnings were anemic, and all that debt was like a parasite sucking the life out of the company. Remember, falling revenues and mounting debt almost always lead to one fatal outcome: bankruptcy. DNDN was below $10 when I shorted it; I couldn't imagine a scenario where it didn't drop all the way to zero.

In late 2013, I predicted Dendreon's demise in an article for the popular investing site Seeking Alpha. The backlash on the site from the company's proponents was severe and severely misinformed. Some indignant respondents disputed my conclusions by touting the news that Provenge had recently been approved for sale in Europe. Of course, they didn't mention that its two better-performing competitors were also fast on their way to gaining the same approval. Others repeated rumors of an imminent Dendreon buyout by a larger competitor. This line of argument was even less convincing. I am fully aware that approved cancer treatments are rare and thus immensely valuable commodities. But what company in its right mind would take on more than $600 million in debt, on top of retiring hundreds of millions in shareholder equity, for the rights to a poorly selling drug, especially one competing with two cheaper and more popular alternatives? Moreover, as I pointed out in the article, the patent on Provenge would likely be sold during bankruptcy proceedings for a fraction of the cost of buying out the whole company.

The litany of excuses, rationalizations, and hopeful predictions of Dendreon's recovery didn't stop there. People claimed that its treatment would soon be prescribed for numerous new off-label indications. They bashed its competitors as less effective. Most dispiritingly, they blamed contrary investors like me for dragging down the price of the stock. One spelling-challenged commenter even declared that all short-sellers should be "ivicerated." This is a tried-and-true tradition on Wall Street. When things go wrong, investors and corporate executives alike love to blame that old bogeyman, short-sellers. It's a convenient way to justify unwise investments and deflect attention from the real reason companies lose value: the poor decisions of the people running them. Instead of looking inward and redirecting a business's strategy, this scapegoating allows leaders and shareholders the illusion of shedding their own responsibility for the condition of their firms. It's another hollow excuse, like Mark blaming a contraction in monetary policy for Consilium's struggles.

If anything, smart managements should *welcome* short-sellers, because when someone shorts a stock, they are committing themselves to buying it in the future. Unless a company goes bankrupt and its stock price goes to zero, short-sellers have to cover their positions at some point, and if that stock rises in the meantime, their purchases will only push the price higher. Also, as I discussed earlier, short-selling carries an infinite amount of risk. The most you can lose from buying a stock is its share price. Shorting a stock has no such floor. For that reason, short-sellers are almost always the smartest, the most savvy, and also the most *cautious* investors out there. If we weren't, we'd all be broke. And contrary to popular opinion, we don't target companies based on malice, and we don't delight in the near ubiquity of failure in the business world. We simply acknowledge how common failure is and invest accordingly.

TICKER SHOCK

Ironically, I've found that one of the main ways corporate leaders can harm their business is by worrying about its stock too much, either by blaming external factors like short-sellers for its underperformance or by basing strategic decisions on how Wall Street will react to them. Seeing as I make my money almost exclusively on equities, you might think I would want the CEOs of the companies I own to concentrate on nothing but their share prices, but the opposite is true.

Bill Gates is famously disinterested in the performance of Microsoft's stock. He even delayed bringing the company public for several years because he worried that doing so would create a distraction for himself and his employees. "People get confused because the stock price doesn't reflect your financial performance," he told *Fortune* magazine after the company's IPO. "And to have a stock trader call up the chief executive and ask him questions is uneconomic—the ball bearings shouldn't be asking the driver about the grease."*

Most successful executives I've met have been like Gates. They've been too wrapped up in driving the operations of their businesses to pay much attention to the ball bearings and the grease of the stock market. In contrast, the brilliant documentary *Enron: The Smartest Guys in the Room* showed that "ticker shock" infected the highest reaches of that doomed company's management. Its stock quotes were even displayed in the elevators of the corporate headquarters. Enron's executives became so focused on its share price, they were willing to do whatever it

---

*Bro Uttal, "Inside the Deal that Made Bill Gates $350,000,000," *Fortune,* July 21, 1986.

took to boost it higher, even if it meant risking ruin. Many of the leaders of the dead companies walking I've met with have been similarly preoccupied.

Way back before I started my hedge fund, I paid a visit to a strange and short-lived retailer based in Tampa, Florida, called Silk Greenhouse. The company specialized in leasing out bankrupt grocery store locations and stocking their aisles with thousands of fake flowers. Believe it or not, it made a lot of money hawking those imitation roses and carnations. For a little while, its stock shot up past $20. I'll never forget my trip to Silk Greenhouse's corporate headquarters. For one thing, I got hopelessly lost trying to find it. They were so far out in the sticks, I don't think the street they were on was even marked, and after driving in circles for the better part of an hour, I finally figured out why—the industrial park where Silk Greenhouse kept its offices was at the end of a dirt road! But that isn't why I'm talking about the company, even though it makes me laugh to think back on that day (and how flabbergasted I was to discover that this hot company that all of Wall Street was buzzing about was housed at the end of an unpaved street).

Silk Greenhouse was my first experience with a management team that seemed to care about its share price to the exclusion of everything else. I was confronted with evidence of this fixation right away. In the lobby of its offices, I was shocked to see a sign with my name on it: "Welcome to Silk Greenhouse, Scott Fearon!" Underneath that pleasant, if unexpected, greeting was a single piece of information: the company's most recent stock quote. The only thing I remember about my meeting with Silk Greenhouse's CFO was that he spent the whole time talking excitedly about how fast the business was expanding. He pulled out a map of all the locations they had opened around the Southeast since going public and all the new locations they were already in the process of opening. To him, this rapid expansion was the cure-all for everything.

"You're a relatively new business," I pointed out. "Don't you think you should fine-tune your existing locations to make sure they're profitable before buying up as many new ones as you can?"

He dismissed my question with a friendly wave of his hand and confidently predicted that the company's earnings per share would continue to blossom as new Silk Greenhouse outlets sprouted up throughout the region. He also made sure to emphasize the positive effects this aggressive growth would have on its stock price. In the short term, he was right. The stock continued to do well. But hypergrowth—as I later saw with Value Merchants, Building Materials Holding Corporation, and dozens of other companies—can be deadly. Silk Greenhouse's management went too fast, too soon. They tried to open over two dozen new locations virtually at the same time.

It takes time and effort to build out, stock, and staff one large new store, let alone more than twenty of them. Anybody who's ever remodeled a single room in their house knows that construction projects can be full of unexpected delays and cost overruns. Multiply that exponentially, and you've got a good idea of what caused Silk Greenhouse's demise. Planned openings were pushed back repeatedly, new inventory had to be warehoused, and the costs of the expansion kept going up while revenue growth slowed and then finally collapsed.* Eventually, investors got wise and Silk Greenhouse's stock slipped, too. As so often happens, it went down a lot faster than it had gone up. The company was bankrupt less than two years after my trip to Tampa.

---

*"Turning Silk Greenhouse into a Sow's Ear," *Businessweek,* March 17, 1991.

Building Materials Holding Corporation also raised revenues in large part through mergers and acquisitions. In the late 1990s and early 2000s, BMHC steadily bought out smaller competing companies. But as I said earlier, this process also fattened up another part of its balance sheet, its debt load. By the time the housing market turned, Rob and the other BMHC executives had saddled the company with hundreds of millions in liabilities to fund these constant acquisitions. Without that onerous debt load, BMHC might have been able to weather the downturn. But, instead, the company was like someone with a massive credit card bill who suddenly loses their job. With fewer and fewer revenues coming in, it couldn't even afford the minimum payments on its debts and wound up with no better option than bankruptcy.

Growth through acquisitions can be a successful strategy if it is carefully conducted. Airlines, for example, have fairly stable administrative costs, so gaining new routes by buying up competing firms often boosts revenues without adding much more overhead. In many cases, though, growth through acquisitions can be just as dangerous as the kind of expansion-on-steroids that killed off Silk Greenhouse or Value Merchants. While building out and opening a number of new facilities in a short period of time is risky, at least it's an internally managed endeavor. A business's existing employees can, in theory, oversee the process and ensure that it's running smoothly. But integrating a separate business into your own is, by its nature, an outside-in process. For that reason, it's bound to be a crapshoot. No matter how many lawyers and auditors an acquiring company hires, no matter how much due diligence it performs beforehand, the seller almost always gets a better deal than the buyer. Sellers know where the bodies are buried in their businesses, and there's usually a good reason why they're willing to give up ownership.

During the 2000s, Hewlett Packard went on a prolonged acquisition spree. One of its most infamous acquisitions was the mobile device firm Palm. HP wanted to get into the smartphone business and was willing to pay good money to do it—the Palm buyout cost the tech giant $1.2 billion. What did they get for all that cash? A dead company walking whose industry had long left it behind. After multiple visits to Palm's Silicon Valley headquarters, I had shorted its stock, and I was stunned when HP bought such a clearly troubled company. Back in the late 1990s and early 2000s, Palm products, especially its Pilot, were ubiquitous. But HP didn't acquire Palm until 2010, several years after the iPhone and other competitors like Android had crushed Palm's market share. Barely a year after the deal went through, HP shuttered the company and wrote off almost its entire investment.*

The thing that gets lost in all the hype over growth through acquisitions is the effect it can have on morale. People are always a business's most valuable assets, and one of the surest ways to kill that value is to tick employees off by disrupting their lives or making them feel unappreciated. I once played golf with an executive whose previous employer, a large tech company, had gone through a major merger. I asked him how he and his colleagues had handled the transition. He shrugged and said, "We rested and vested." When I asked him to explain what that meant, he told me that almost all of the original employees at his firm felt alienated by the new corporate culture and planned on quitting, but not until their stock options in the newly merged company vested.

---

*Pete Carey, "HP's Acquisition Misstep Far from the First," *San Jose Mercury News,* November 20, 2012.

"For a whole year, we did the bare minimum to keep from getting fired and then we were gone," he recounted. "It was actually quite nice. I went home at five every day. I saw my wife and kids a lot. I played golf three, four times a week."

Andrew Carnegie has been quoted as saying, "The only irreplaceable capital an organization possesses is the knowledge and ability of its people." Too many high-level executives overlook this fact and underestimate how important employee morale is. They assume that they can mix and match peoples' jobs, or move people seamlessly from one role to another, or even demote them to lower positions without any negative consequences. Then they wonder why their companies aren't growing or producing as much anymore.

A little over a decade ago, the so-called Four Horsemen of San Francisco investment banks—Hambrecht & Quist, Montgomery Securities, Robertson Stephens, and the Baltimore-based Alex. Brown & Sons—were each bought out by major financial conglomerates. These were all boutique but immensely profitable brokerages, and each fetched a massive buyout price. The big banks that acquired them assumed all those profits would magically shift over to their balance sheets. But what made the Four Horsemen great weren't figures on accounting statements. It was the people and the culture that they had formed over the years. Each had a small number of smart, highly motivated employees who routinely put in 60- and 80-hour weeks. After getting swallowed up into giant, far-flung corporations like J.P. Morgan and Bank of America, many of those employees failed to take to their new bosses. They lost motivation and focus, and a large number of them took their expertise and their energies elsewhere. As a result, all four of those acquisitions wound up being huge money losers.

M&A, INC.

Mergers and acquisitions are definitely risky methods for growth, but one party always makes a profit on them: the banks who facilitate the deals.

Most acquisitions in the corporate world begin with a phone call from an investment banker. They'll dial up executives and drop hints that another company might be interested in being acquired for the right amount. Then they'll hype the potential benefits of the deal. The word that gets thrown around the most in these pitches is that old standby, *synergies.* As I mentioned earlier, this is one of the most trite and overused terms in business and investing. When I hear people mouthing it about a given company or companies, I frequently use that as a signal to study those companies further—not as potential investments but as stocks I might consider shorting.

Investors frequently make the same mistake as merger-happy managements. They get so mesmerized by breathless headlines in the business media about acquisitions that they forget to turn the page on a company's financial statements and evaluate whether countervailing factors like rising debt actually make such deals worth the costs. They also fail to evaluate whether proposed mergers actually make basic business sense. I was shocked when many respectable analysts praised the potential deal between Blockbuster and Hollywood Video. And yet Wall Street churned out all sorts of optimistic reports cheering the merger's potential. The same thing happens all the time with companies caught up in the flawed formula of hypergrowth. They tout their aggressive plans for expansion, and stock buyers jump at the prospects of new revenues. But, as with Silk Greenhouse, those promised new revenues can easily fail to materialize. For these reasons, I generally prefer to invest in companies that grow organically, at a reasonable pace. It might be a slower, less flashy process. But it almost always means less risk and more profit in the long run.

SEVEN

SHORT TO LONG

Rescuing Failing Companies

History does *nothing, it "possesses* no *immense wealth," it "wages* no *battles."*
It is man, *real, living man who does all that, who possesses and fights; "his-*
tory" is not, as it were, a person apart, using man as a means to achieve its own
aims; history is nothing but *the activity of man pursuing his aims.*

—Karl Marx

Don't shoot the messenger; analyze the message.

—Anonymous

DESPITE THIS BOOK'S FOCUS ON FAILURE IN BUSINESS, I
have not made all or even most of my money from short-selling. As I've
said, I am not a "perma-bear." I don't consistently short the markets and
hope that they will fall. I am a classic hedge fund manager in that I make
both short and long investments. And even though I haven't talked about
it much, I spend just as much time, if not more, seeking out companies

to invest in for the long term as I do scouting failures on their way to bankruptcy.

The key is flexibility. I try not to have a rigid view of things. I assess the numbers, I meet with management teams, and I do my best to make the correct call on a given stock, whether that means shorting it, buying it, or holding off. Sometimes I hit a home run. Sometimes I lose. But I always do everything I can to stay open-minded and willing to adapt to new information or circumstances. I believe this mental limberness is why my fund has consistently earned good returns, even though it has lived through some of the most volatile and unproductive business cycles in generations. Look at the 2000s. The stock market—after two massive collapses—was essentially flat for the entire decade. And yet my fund, even with a calamitous 2009 (which I will talk about later), managed to rise more than 100 percent after all fees during that lost decade for US stocks.

I'm not bringing up these numbers to tout my success or pump up my ego. I'm doing it because, so far, I have probably failed to emphasize something that I deeply believe: *failure might be more common than people like to admit, but it is not inevitable—even when things look irreversibly dire.* I know I've presented numerous examples of smart people (including myself) making poor decisions. But the reality is that skillful leadership can, and often does, stave off disaster.

In late 2013, on a business trip to New York, I was lucky enough to see famed fund manager Stephen Mandel give a talk to a group of visiting MBA students from my graduate alma mater, Northwestern. Mandel very generously shared some of the hard-earned lessons he'd learned over the decades he'd been in the investment business. Right at the top of his list was a very pithy maxim: "Managements matter." Too many investors, he explained, get so lost in the weeds of a company's financial results—recent earnings, projections, extrapolations, and other purely mathematical data—that they forget to study the thing that makes any company great (or terrible): the people running it. He called this fixation on evaluating numbers instead of flesh-and-blood managers going "Excel crazy." As I listened to Mandel, I was taken back to my early days in Houston working under Geoff Raymond. He would constantly chide me for burying my head too deeply in financial disclosures and earnings reports.

"Get up and go outside, Scott," he'd tell me. "You'll learn more in five minutes of talking to someone at a company than you will in a week crunching its numbers."

Both Geoff Raymond and Stephen Mandel were well aware that the wrong management team can ruin the most profitable, well-conceived business. On the other hand, they understood that the right set of executives can bring mediocre or even desperately ill companies back to health. In my own career, I've seen plenty of corporate managers recognize the troubles they were facing and make the necessary choices to pull their businesses out of the fire. And I'm not talking about draconian, Frank Lorenzo–style turnarounds, either. Unlike Lorenzo, the executives that have impressed me the most have managed to avoid bankruptcy. And, also unlike Lorenzo, they have set their companies up for long-term health and success. A couple of times, these rescues have been so effective, I've even covered my short positions and turned around and bought the stocks involved. In other words, I've profited on the same company's descent *and* recovery.

A BAZAAR STORY

Ever since Geoff Raymond and I drove out to see Jerry at Global Marine way back in 1984, I've visited scores of corporate management teams each year. All told, I've interviewed executives at more than 1,400 company headquarters since I started my hedge fund over twenty years ago. Often, I'll go back to the same company repeatedly, even if I don't own their stock, just so I can keep an eye on what they're up to. This is especially true for companies in the Bay Area. I talked about Cygnus Therapeutics earlier. I dropped by its offices in Redwood City five times in eight years and never bought or shorted a single share of its stock. I figured I had no excuse for not keeping up with such a potentially great business that was in my backyard. And I felt the same way about a very different kind of company on the other side of the bay.

Every year or two for more than a decade, I've driven across the Richmond–San Rafael Bridge to Oakland to spend some time with the people in charge of Cost Plus World Market (stock symbol: CPWM). Its headquarters near Jack London Square are housed in a drab, single-story building underneath an overpass of the 880 freeway. The area's gentrified a bit since I first started going there, with some modern-looking condo towers going up nearby, but it's still primarily an industrial and warehouse district. One of my favorite barbecue joints, Everett and Jones, is a few blocks away. I usually pick up a plate of ribs on my way home.

Long before I became a money manager, I had a personal connection to Cost Plus. My father used to bring my brother and me along to San Francisco when he attended conferences there, and I have fond memories of walking from our hotel in Union Square through Chinatown and into the original Cost Plus location in Fisherman's Wharf. That original location—which opened way back in the 1950s—was the first major treasure hunt retailer, and it was as much of a destination in San Francisco as Coit Tower or Golden Gate Park. Stepping through the doors was like going on a mini round-the-world tour. I can still smell the mix of teak and wood oil and wicker. You never knew what you'd find. It had exotic but inexpensive Asian furniture, weird crackers from Denmark, tins of Iranian caviar, handmade soap from Mexico. It was a complete grab bag. It was also the first American retailer to import cheap but high-quality wines from places like Chile and Australia.

Given my nostalgia for Cost Plus, when it came public in the mid-1990s and started opening new outlets around the country, I was tempted to buy its stock. Unfortunately, so was everyone else. Buoyed by the crazy bull market of the dotcom mania, CPWM was already trading at $44 by the time I made my first trip to the company's headquarters in 1999—on a mere 66 cents a share in trailing earnings. That's a whopping multiple of *sixty-seven* if you're scoring at home. (Remember, the multiples of Costco and Starbucks that scared me off of those companies were only in the thirties.) On top of that, no less than ten different analysts from major brokerages were hyping Cost Plus as a buy. I refused to join the herd given this sky-high valuation. But I continued to travel over the bridge every year or two for a plate of ribs and a meeting with Cost Plus's management. That persistence wound up making me a lot of money, in unexpected ways.

Not surprisingly, holding off on CPWM initially was a good decision. When the dotcom mania evaporated, the stock sank with the rest of the market. Within two years, it had bottomed out at $18. By the time I went back to Oakland in July 2003, however, the post 9/11 recession had ended and CPWM was back up to $40 again. The company had just hired a new chief financial officer, a friendly, stocky guy named John. I got to know John fairly well over the next few years, because I did in fact become very interested in Cost Plus as a potential investment. It was starting to look more and more like a dead company walking.

For one, Cost Plus appeared to be subscribing to the risky formula of hypergrowth. It was up to 175 stores by 2003, and John told me management was planning to expand to 600 total in the near future. Even more troubling, I began to notice a shift in the way the company was doing business. Cost Plus got caught up in the housing mania of the time and started stocking more high-end home furniture and fewer quirky knick-knacks. As a result, its stores didn't have the same *feel*. The only way I can think to explain it is that they just weren't all that much fun anymore. Walking into a Cost Plus wasn't like walking into the eclectic bazaar I remembered from my childhood. It was more like walking into an Ethan Allen showroom. As a longtime (almost *lifelong*) fan of the chain's treasure hunt atmosphere, I suspected that the company's management had decided to stop appealing to people like me. They seemed to want to attract a different, "better" kind of consumer. This was right around the time I was about to close my first restaurant, which meant I had just lived through a painful, firsthand lesson in how dangerous it can be to misread or alienate your core customer base—and Cost Plus's leaders seemed like they were doing just that.

The company's numbers only heightened this suspicion. Its "comps"—same-store sales—were still growing year over year but at a slower clip. And while the average amount customers were spending (known as its "ticket") was creeping higher, its "counts" were down, meaning there were fewer and fewer of those customers to speak of. Finally, its "turns"—the number of times individual items in its inventory sold out and were restocked—were dropping, too. That all made sense to me. If you're stocking $800 luxury couches instead of funky $25 end tables, you're going to move less inventory. The kicker for me, though, was the wine selection. When I came back to interview John again in

2004, he proudly informed me that Cost Plus was about to start stocking fine wines from Napa and France. He seemed genuinely surprised by my negative reaction.

"People can get a thirty-dollar Napa Cabernet or a forty-dollar Bordeaux anywhere," I explained. "That's not what you guys are about. You're about that great six-dollar Malbec from Argentina or that sweet eight-dollar Riesling from some obscure vintner in Australia. That's why people have always gone to your stores, to find interesting, inexpensive things they can't find anywhere else. Now you're offering them the exact opposite. You're giving them boring stuff that costs more money!"

John defended the move with some data about consumer trends. But I didn't buy it. I decided I was going to watch Cost Plus a lot more closely in the coming months. If its leaders kept up with this new strategy of offering more conventional and expensive goods, I was sure its results would continue to suffer and its stock price would inevitably fall.

And fall it did.

By my next visit in August 2005, the company's comps had turned negative and its stock was down to $20, half of where it had been only two years earlier. During that meeting, John offered a whole raft of excuses for the poor results, including the costs of various promotions they had run, the severance package they had paid to their recently departed CEO, and even something he called "the Walmart effect."

"Walmart?" I asked incredulously. "You're not even in their sector, John. The economy's booming. Consumer spending is at record levels, and almost every retailer in the country is thriving. You guys are the exception. Don't you think your problems might be *internal?*"

John was silent for a moment. It seemed like he might have been considering my point. But then he quickly started back into the same explanations he'd already offered. I realized he was playing the same "blame game" I've seen executives at troubled businesses engage in for my entire career. His Walmart effect argument in particular reminded me of the CFO of Consilium citing fluctuations in the M-1 money supply for his company's problems, or the unseasonable weather excuses apparel companies perpetually give for disappointing sales, or the sluggish economy line all sorts of businesses put into their financial disclosures to paper over their issues. I didn't begrudge John for trying to deflect responsibility, though. He obviously didn't make the disastrous decision to turn a once vibrant, unique brand into just another stale luxury goods shop. He was just a loyal executive doing his best to put a good face on a clearly bad-and-getting-worse situation.

I left that meeting determined to short Cost Plus if it dipped below $10. It took a little while but it did so early in 2007. I waited a few more months to make sure the downward trend continued, I pulled the trigger when CPWM hit $8. By February 2009, only twenty months later, the stock was down to 50 cents, and I was about as certain as I've ever been that it was heading all the way to zero. But, as with so many of my other assumptions in 2009, I was wrong. Very wrong. Out of nowhere, the stock started to creep up again. By September 2009, it was close to two bucks. I couldn't figure out what was going on, so I got back in my car and crossed the bridge over to Oakland. The company had installed a new CFO since my last visit. Her name was Jane, and she turned out to be one of the most knowledgeable and transparent executives I have ever met.

Jane had been promoted from within the company right around the time I shorted its stock. She was young and very bright. She was also refreshingly frank about the state of affairs at Cost Plus. She didn't blame the company's woes on Walmart or marketing promotions or even the latest recession. Without any prompting or obfuscations, she freely admitted that its problems had been entirely self-inflicted.

"We messed up," she said flatly. "We made a terrible mistake and now we're paying for it. But it's not too late to turn things around. We've still got access to capital, and we're in the process of returning to what made us successful in the first place—highly original products from around the world."

"So the treasure hunt formula is coming back?" I asked.

"It's already back," she replied with a smile. "We've cut out high-end furniture altogether, and we've increased our emphasis on lower-priced gifts and consumables. Now we're just hoping that our customers will continue to come back, too."

"What about the recession?"

Jane laughed. "We've been in our own personal recession for years now, Scott. You've been coming here regularly for a long time. You know we've been struggling to keep our heads above water. So really, we're in a better position than a lot of other retailers. We've already closed our worst-performing stores, and we've made the strategic changes to be competitive in this environment. Everyone else is just now starting that process and trying to catch up."

She proceeded to list, from memory, the latest sales numbers to back up her assertions. I never saw her glance at her notes once. Cost Plus was already seeing an increase in the number of customers coming into its stores. Turns were going up, as well. To top it off, Jane showed me that, even after all its troubles, the company still had access to a large line of credit that it had arranged years earlier and had never come close to exhausting. That might have been the most impressive piece of data she shared. Probably more than any other industry, retailers desperately rely on lines of credit. Without them, they can't stock their stores or pay their expenses. The fact that Jane and the rest of Cost Plus's leadership had safeguarded its credit while so many others were being frozen out by the banks finally proved to me that the company had a decent shot at staying out of bankruptcy.

As I strolled out of Jane's office, I began to worry that my Cost Plus investment was in trouble, and that I, too, had better start thinking about shifting strategy. I covered my positions in four different trades during the first half of 2010. CPWM was already up to $3.50 by the middle of that year, and it didn't show any signs of stopping. At the same time, the number of Wall Street analysts who were covering the stock had dropped from well over a dozen just a few years earlier to exactly one—and he was still giving Cost Plus a negative rating. In other words, the company was in the opposite position it had been in when I first started visiting its headquarters in 1999. Back then, it was the darling of the retail sector, with a whole chorus of analysts singing its praises. As a result, its share price had been bloated beyond what its earnings merited. But now that it had been forgotten by Wall Street, Cost Plus's stock was starting to look like the Chilean wines it was famous for first bringing into the country— a tasty and underrated bargain.

As is my habit, though, I didn't rush to buy. I waited to see how the company fared during 2010's holiday season. That hesitancy cost me a few dollars. The stock was near $8—almost exactly the amount at which I had shorted it four years earlier—when I finally started buying. Cost Plus had posted good holiday sales, and the rest of its numbers continued impress, too. In early 2012, it announced another strong Christmas season and the stock rose into the high teens. Then, in May, the company's board accepted a buyout offer from Bed Bath & Beyond (stock symbol: BBBY) for $22 a share.

As I've said repeatedly, failure in business (and in investing) happens more frequently than success. Acknowledging that fact instead of pretending it isn't true has helped me make a lot of money. But finding great companies to invest in over the long term is still my bread and butter—and for good reason. Going long on successful businesses will always be the best way to earn outsized returns.

My experience with Cost Plus bears this out. All told, after waiting three years for it to go to zero before I finally covered my position, I made about $1 million shorting its stock. That's not a bad return. But when I bought the same amount of stock as I had shorted (225,000 shares), I netted more than $3 million in just over a year. That's triple the money in a third of the time—and even that is a relatively modest profit when it comes to successful longs. Think about how much I would have earned on Costco and Starbucks if I had bought their stocks after my trip to Seattle in 1992. We're talking about once-in-a-career-type investments that doubled and doubled and doubled again many times over. You just don't make that kind of money on shorts. There's a fixed number between a stock price and zero, and that's as much as you're going to get out of those positions. For long investments, however, there is no such limit.

The people who bought in early on one of the most stunning and successful corporate turnarounds in recent history, Apple, know how profitable long investments can be. Actually, Apple has come back from the dead several times in its history. But its most impressive revival came after Steve Jobs took the company away from what had been its core business for decades, the personal computer. First, he reinvented how consumers bought, listened to, and shared music with the iPod. Then, a few years later, he turned cellular phones into *Star Trek*–level computing devices with the iPhone. Of course, Jobs has already been praised to the moon for these ingenious inventions—as well as the iPad, the last of his revolutionary advances before his death—but it's hard to overstate how bold he was in bringing these devices to market.

The vast majority of corporate leaders spend their energies inventing reasons *not* to change. Even when faced with clear—you could even say Blockbuster-sized—evidence that they have miscalculated or that the old ways aren't going to work anymore, they willfully don blinders while the rest of their industry shifts around them. Apple could have continued to rely on PC sales, like its competitors Dell and Gateway did, and it probably would have muddled along in its niche. Instead, Jobs took the company into not one but two completely new sectors and transformed Apple into the largest tech company in the world.

I wasn't smart enough to buy Apple before its stock took off in the mid-2000s and went from $50 to almost $800 a share a few years later, but I've had my share of wildly successful longs. Once in the bluest of blue moons, you climb into a stock, strap yourself in, and hold on for dear life as it rockets up into the stratosphere. I'm not like the newsletter writers or promoters on cable television who try to act like those kinds of winners are everywhere. They're not. But if you do this long enough and you know what to look for, you can find them.

A TARNISHED GEM

The reasons for Cost Plus's decline should be familiar if you've read this far in the book. Its previous leadership committed a whopping four of the six business sins I look for in dead companies walking. First, they

GOING LONG

Since the financial crisis of 2008, I've had to adjust my investment approach toward more long investments. I still look for dead companies walking, but my fund is weighted far more on the long side now. Short selling just isn't as profitable anymore, and there are four primary reasons why.

First, because of fewer IPOs and a continuing trend of public companies going private, the number of US stocks over $1 a share shrank from over seven thousand in the late 1990s to under five thousand by early 2014. Second, Sarbanes-Oxley and other new regulations have reduced the number of companies using aggressive accounting. That means there are not only fewer public companies in the market these days, there aren't that many potential frauds to sell short, either. Third, with the Federal Reserve shrinking interest rates to goose the economy, prime brokerages began to charge short-sellers a daily "negative rebate fee" to make up for the interest the brokerages used to earn by reinvesting the proceeds of short sales. In 2013 alone, my fund paid more than $2 million in these fees. Short selling is already a very risky activity. Paying millions just for the right to potentially lose millions more makes it downright perilous.

Finally, people in my business have simply gotten better at their jobs. The number of hedge funds hunting for short ideas has exploded, as most managers justify their high performance fees on the basis they can add value (and protect capital) using both shorts and longs. Not only that, hedge fund managers are a lot smarter nowadays than they were when I started out. That means the competition for the handful of good shorts is intense.

got caught up in the housing mania and abandoned the treasure hunt atmosphere that had defined the brand's identity. Second, in a move that could be seen as a smaller prelude to JCPenney's disastrous firing of its own customers in 2012, they alienated Cost Plus's core customer base by killing off that eclectic atmosphere and stocking more expensive and slow-selling furniture. Third, they followed the flawed formula of hypergrowth, opening too many stores too quickly. And finally, when they were confronted with clear evidence of the negative consequences of these strategies, they cast around for external factors to blame instead of recognizing their own culpability.

Even one of these misguided decisions could have damaged the business enough to sink it, but all four together made bankruptcy seem inevitable. Throw in the fact that at the same time Jane and its other new managers were trying to repair the company, the wider economy was mired in the worst supercycle recession in almost a century, and Cost Plus's recovery starts to look almost miraculous. But there was nothing supernatural about its return to success. It was just a matter of an executive team taking responsibility and making better choices. Sure, they did so at the last possible moment before the company went under. (We're not just talking the eleventh hour. It was more like the eleventh hour and fifty-nine minutes. Remember, shares of Cost Plus were trading for pocket change at the stock's low point.) But that just goes to show how effective smart, clear-eyed, and personally engaged leadership can be.

Another corporate Lazarus that I was lucky enough to discover made many of the same mistakes Cost Plus did and brought itself just as close to bankruptcy. For most of its long history, the jewelry retailer Zale Corporation (stock symbol: ZLC)—known as "America's Diamond Store"—had earned the majority of its revenues on bridal jewelry like diamond engagement rings and other exclusive merchandise. The company didn't target the same wealthy buyers as Tiffany. Most of its stores were, and still are, in shopping malls. They were places where predominantly middle-class consumers went to buy loved ones tokens of their devotion, often by using the company's branded store credit card. But in the mid-2000s, right around the time Cost Plus's management decided to turn its quirky bazaars into luxury furniture showrooms, the leaders of Zale inexplicably went the opposite direction—they shifted the company's inventory to include a much broader assortment of inexpensive, kitschy items.

The industry term for these kinds of lower-end pieces is "fashion jewelry," but it would have been a stretch to call most of what Zale was offering jewelry. *Baubles* was a more fitting word. (One of its lines was Hello Kitty–branded tchotchkes like bejeweled iPhone cases.) Compounding this already questionable business move, the company attempted to make up for the lower margins these kinds of items earned by following the dreaded hypergrowth formula. It expanded its number of locations aggressively, betting that higher sales volumes would bring higher profits, too.

Zale's switch to cheaper trinkets worked about as well as Cost Plus's attempt to go upscale—meaning, it didn't work at all. The new merchandise put off the brand's core, middle-class customers. Even before the economic meltdown of 2008, same-store comps were dropping and operating margins were following suit. Nonetheless, the company's leaders forged ahead with their "value-oriented" strategy, and things went from bad to worse. After a disappointing holiday season in 2007, they tried to clear a massive backlog in unsold inventory by staging prolonged clearance sales, offering deep discounts on already discounted merchandise. These efforts only dragged profits lower, not to mention the company's share price. ZLC declined by more than two-thirds in 2007, from the high twenties to the mid-teens. At the end of 2008, as the interminable Great Recession was only beginning to set in, ZLC was a $3 stock. The company lost almost $200 million in fiscal 2009, and its share price dipped below $1. Meanwhile, its debt swelled to almost $500 million. By the time the board of directors cleaned house and brought in a fresh management team in January 2010—after yet another rotten Christmas season—America's Diamond Store was looking extremely rough.

New CEO Theo Killion made some immediate improvements. He began to close many of the company's unprofitable locations. He also cleared as much low-priced fashion jewelry from the remaining stores as he could. Those moves, plus a critical cash infusion from a private equity firm, kept the company from going all the way under—in the short term, at least. When I first visited Zale headquarters in Irving, Texas, in November 2011, its stock had crawled back over $3. But it was still a long way from being anything close to a profitable concern. Its debt load was still enormous, it was still losing money, and the all-important Christmas season was looming. Without a good holiday quarter, ZLC could have very easily turned into a lump of coal after all. Nonetheless, I sensed an almost giddy energy in the two executives I interviewed, the newly hired CFO Tom and the head of investor relations, Roxane.

"We've closed more than forty of our worst-performing stores, and we've had four straight quarters of positive same-store comps," they told me excitedly, almost talking over each other. "And we've just announced an exclusive agreement with Vera Wang to sell her designer bridal jewelry."

Most of my meetings with corporate executives are pretty drab affairs. Chief financial officers aren't generally known for their rah-rah enthusiasm, which is why that first visit with Roxane and Tom stands out in my mind. Sitting across from them as they ticked off one positive data point after another, I almost felt like I was attending a corporate pep rally. Don't get me wrong; they were quite poised and professional, and nothing they claimed was inaccurate, but they were clearly happy to come to work every day. It took me a little while to realize what I was sensing in them: pride. It was obvious from their attitudes that they were extremely proud to be a part of the company's turnaround, and who could blame them? They and their fellow executives were doing everything they could to save an iconic, even historic, American brand. Zale had been around for almost ninety years. It had survived the Great Depression, World War II, and countless other ups and downs. To hear them talk, it was going to make it through its latest and most severe crisis, too.

Nonetheless, there was no way I was going near the stock. Not yet. Despite Tom and Roxane's infectious optimism, I'd heard too many executives at troubled companies cheerfully predict imminent recovery, only to see them file for bankruptcy a short while later. As I drove back from Zale's offices back to downtown Dallas, I was hopeful the company would recover. But I was far from convinced that it would.

Fortunately, that skepticism didn't cost me very much money.

I didn't make it back to Irving, Texas, for almost a year and a half. ZLC was still below $5 at that point, but the company was obviously well on its way to something it hadn't enjoyed for half a decade: profitability.

Roxane smiled as she led me into her office and happily rattled off another laundry list of positive developments. The company had now seen *ten* straight quarters of positive comps. It had closed another several dozen unprofitable stores and was actually starting to consider opening a few new ones. Best of all, the previous holiday season had gone even better than expected, and the company's exclusive Vera Wang and Celebration diamond collections were now responsible for almost 15 percent of its revenues and counting. That last detail impressed me the most, because it demonstrated that Zale's leadership was not just trying to reverse the bad decisions of the previous management team, they were also committed to something that even executives at thriving concerns usually have a hard time accomplishing—innovation.

In the midst of lean times, most businesses assume the corporate equivalent of the fetal position. This usually means draconian cutbacks, layoffs, and asset protection. Zale had definitely done its share of cost cutting by closing as many unprofitable stores as it had. A lot of analysts gloss over how difficult that process can be. It's extremely arduous to shutter so many locations. But that wasn't what convinced me to buy a big chunk of stock in the company after my second visit. Slashing expenses was necessary for Zale to recover. But what made me believe that its stock was undervalued was management's determination to grow profits by investing in new products with better margins. Instead of sourcing cheap fashion jewelry from outside vendors, it was now actively creating and marketing high-quality, in-store collections. These not only earned Zale higher returns, they vastly strengthened the overall brand.

Consumers, even middle- and working-class consumers, do not want the jewelry store where they buy their wedding bands or other cherished items to seem like a glorified trinket shop. They want to feel like they are getting a good price, but they also want to believe that the products they are investing in are as special and lasting as the devotion they feel for their loved ones. Diamonds are supposed to be forever, and it's hard to feel like you're wearing something timeless when you picked it out of a clearance case next to a Hello Kitty keychain. Unlike the previous regime, Zale's new management obviously understood that essential aspect of their business, and they were willing to invest in repairing the brand's image by stocking quality new products.

I also appreciated that Zale had adopted what amounted to an anti-hypergrowth strategy for its recovery. The company was paying down debt, closing unprofitable stores, and doing everything it could to boost profit margins. It had even signed a new agreement for an in-house credit card, which would save it up to 2 percent on one-third of all transactions. (The previous management had inexplicably outsourced its credit card business to Citibank.) Thanks to these measures and its commitment to growing its own exclusive product lines, its gross margin had surpassed 50 percent for the first time in years by the time of my first visit. Five months later, when the company announced its full fiscal year results, those margins were at record levels. Combined with its debt repayment and other cost reductions, Zale showed positive earnings per share and operating margins of almost 2 percent for 2013—not great, but a hell of a lot better than the losses the company had been posting.

ZLC tripled in price in the first six months I owned it, but I never considered selling it. In fact, I bought another large chunk and considered buying more. Why? Because, as Stephen Mandel said, managements matter. I never got a chance to purchase more shares of ZLC, though. In early 2014, the largest jewelry company in the country, Signet (stock symbol: SIG), acquired Zale for $21 a share.

JACKPOT

Zale's commitment to finding new ways to boost its profit margins brought it back from the abyss. By the time the new management team took over, just holding down the fort wasn't going to cut it. The company was in a shambles, and it had to figure out how to build the proverbial airplane in midflight. As I said, innovating is hard enough for successful businesses. Doing it on a shoestring budget while trying to stave off bankruptcy is a Herculean task—but I've seen the best corporate managers pull it off, and not just in retail.

When I first visited the management of the Reno-based slot machine company International Gaming Technology (stock symbol: IGT) in the early 1990s, its headquarters made Cost Plus's modest Oakland offices look like the Taj Majal. The company would eventually move into a gleaming new facility on Prototype Road, but at the time IGT was still housed out among a cluster of low-slung warehouses on a parched strip of land at the edge of Reno-Tahoe International Airport. It didn't seem like a fitting home for a business that was making record profits, thanks to a boom in legalized gambling. Over the previous half decade, Indian casinos had been opening all over the country, and the entire gaming industry was flush because of it. But then again, IGT's stock had been down as low as 11 *cents* only a few years earlier in the mid-1980s, so I assumed that its employees were happy to have any offices at all.

The company's CFO was a linebacker-sized guy named Tom. He had thinning brown hair and a soothing, resonant baritone. After he nearly crimped my palm in half with his handshake, he offered to show me some of the latest machines. I gladly accepted, but before we stepped out of his office, I made the mistake of commenting on one of the numerous framed photos of Harley-Davidsons hanging on the walls. Tom spent a good while regaling me with tales of riding his bikes up into the Sierras. To be honest, it got a little dull. But eventually, he remembered that I was there to talk about slots, not choppers, and he took me out to the lobby of the building, where several dozen of the newest models were on display. He let me try my luck at some Hollywood-themed machines, which featured the characters of old television shows and movies. I gave the *Gilligan's Island* one a spin, but I can't say it did much for me. I've never been a big gambler.

"With all those new Indian casinos being built, your orders must be way up," I said over the electronic chirps and whistles of the slots.

"Absolutely," he agreed. "We're struggling to keep up. But it's a good problem to have."

"You guys must be thanking your lucky stars for legalized gambling. It came just in time for you."

I thought I was making an obvious point, but Tom gave me a perplexed frown.

"What do you mean?" he asked.

"The company was on the brink of bankruptcy in 1986," I recounted. "Your competition was eating up your market share, and your stock was selling for pennies. Then the Supreme Court said that Native Americans could run casinos on their reservations. It saved your business."

Tom visibly bristled at my version of events.

"Respectfully, Scott," he said, "that's not quite accurate. You make it sound like we just got lucky or something. But luck had nothing to do with it. Don't get me wrong; we're happy about all the new casinos opening, and we're making way more money than we would have without them. But that's not what saved us."

"What did?"

"*We* did," he said with a smile. "We spend five times more on research and development than our competitors. That's our edge. We knew there was no way we could compete by cutting costs or trying to make the same machines for less money—we had to come up with something new. So even though we were losing tons of money at the time, we kept investing in R&D and it paid off." He swept his big hand around the room of colorful, jangling consoles. "It used to be that every one of these machines was an isolated unit, with its own odds and payouts. The customer put a coin in, and if they hit, they might win twenty or fifty bucks or maybe even a couple hundred on some of the higher-end models. But now, all of these machines and hundreds of others are linked up electronically so that their jackpots are pooled together. That same customer can put a quarter into one of these slots and win fifty or a hundred thousand dollars, maybe even a million. It's called a progressive jackpot. We put out the first version of it *before* Indian gaming was officially legalized. People were already crazy for it and we had orders pouring in."

Tom led me back to his office again and showed me some numbers to illustrate his point. It was true; IGT's revenues had started growing again before the legalization boom. But I was still dubious about his reasoning.

"How can you say that without legalization you would still be doing well?" I asked. "Sure, you invented progressive slots, and I can see that they were selling well, but there are only so many casinos in Nevada and Atlantic City. Once they all bought the new machines, where would your growth have come from? You're a manufacturer. You need to make new sales and new markets to make money."

Tom didn't answer right away. Instead, he showed me one of the company's balance sheets and jabbed a meaty finger at an item labeled "Casino Operations." I saw that it made up nearly a third of all of IGT's earnings.

"What's this?" I asked.

"The real innovation of progressive slots isn't the machines themselves," Tom asserted. "It's how we distribute them. We don't sell the units outright anymore and take a one-time profit. We lease them to the casinos. That way we get a healthy cut of every coin that goes into them. So even if the boom starts to taper off, which is not going to happen anytime soon, we've still got a major revenue stream coming in."

Tom sat back contentedly in his chair and watched me as I studied IGT's numbers. He could tell that his arguments were sinking in.

I bought my first tranche of IGT shortly after that meeting. The stock had just spilt and risen back up into the mid-thirties. But I wound up buying a lot of more it, and I was glad I did. A couple of years after my meeting with Tom, I was down in Las Vegas talking to the CFO of Mirage Resorts. They had just opened the Treasure Island casino on the Strip, and one of the main selling points the executive used to try to convince me to invest in their company was the fact that they had gone "100 percent IGT" in the slots at the new resort.

"Normally, you want a mix of different machines from different manufacturers," he said. "But our research shows that customers love IGT's products. They go crazy for them, so we decided to give them what they want."

I went home and bought another chunk of shares. Then, a year later, IGT debuted what would become the most popular slot of all time—the *Wheel of Fortune* game—and I bought yet another batch.

It didn't take a stroke of genius to realize that buying stock in a slot machine company in 1993 was probably a good investment. The gaming sector was undergoing an unprecedented expansion. It wasn't just Native Americans fueling the boom, either. Riverboat gambling was growing all over the Midwest and South, and cities like Detroit were preparing to legalize gambling outright. At the same time, slot machines had become hugely popular and were now responsible for as much as 70 percent

SILICON VALLEY EAST

In many ways, the executives of IGT ran the company more like a Silicon Valley tech firm than an old-fashioned slot machine manufacturer. They recognized that their creatives—the designers who dreamed up new kinds of slot machines—were their biggest assets, and they spoiled them as much as Google spoils its employees.

On one of my later trips to Reno, I was walking through the parking lot of IGT's giant new campus with Tom, and we passed a brand-new red Ferrari Spider.

"Who's car is that?" I asked.

"That's Steve's," he said. "He's one of our best developers. I'm shocked to see it here, to be honest. I don't think he's come into the office for a month or so."

of most casinos' revenues. Finally, the general public had become much more accepting of gambling as a pastime. It wasn't viewed as something sinful or unsavory anymore.

Given these factors, it might have seemed like I could have thrown a dart at a list of publicly traded slot machine makers and expected to make good returns. But that wasn't the case. IGT's two largest competitors in the slots industry, Williams Gaming (WMS) and Bally Technologies (BYI), had much lower valuations in the early 1990s. On paper, they might have appeared to have been better investments at the time. But after visiting Reno and speaking with Tom, I decided to bet on IGT, and it was the right play. BYI and WMS wound up not being nearly as lucrative, and the reasons why were familiar.

In the mid-2000s, in the midst of an absolute orgy of housing bubble–driven consumer spending, Cost Plus managed to post poor earnings even as just about every other player in the retail world soaked up massive profits. Despite what its CFO tried to tell me, this didn't happen because of the Walmart effect or some misguided marketing campaigns. It happened for one simple reason: the people in charge of the company *made lousy decisions.* They screwed up, and even a stampeding bull market couldn't save them. The same was true to a lesser extent for Williams and Bally during the 1990s and early 2000s. Neither of them came close to developing products as popular as IGT's, so even as gambling boomed and IGT's stock rose steadily, their share prices lagged behind. BYI even dipped precipitously toward the end of the 1990s, and the company was forced to engineer a reverse stock split.

The thing that separated IGT from Bally and Williams is the same thing that saved Cost Plus and Zale: people—smart, *adaptable* management teams making good decisions. As Tom proudly said, luck had nothing to do with IGT's success. The company's leaders created their own good fortune. In the mid-1980s, they were getting creamed by cheaper competitors. They could have gone the Yellow Pages route and cut costs drastically to try to wring a few drops of profit from an ever-shrinking pot of revenues. Or they could have pulled a Blockbuster and made a few cosmetic changes to their business model. But instead, they spent *more* on their products and aggressively sought out large, game-changing innovations. Like Zale with its Vera Wang collection and other initiatives, IGT's return from the brink of bankruptcy was due to this emphasis on finding creative new ways to boost earnings.

That wound up not only saving the business, but making it the dominant player in its industry.

Cost Plus's new management team didn't come up with a novel new concept or product like IGT and Zale. They didn't have to—the company already had a novel approach that had been proven successful. Nonetheless, going back to its original treasure hunt formula was almost as bold as spending more money on research and development in the midst of a major crisis, as IGT did. During Cost Plus's low ebb, its new managers could have behaved like the people in the paging industry and invented new justifications for why their focus on high-end furniture was eventually going to pay off. But they recognized that the new luxury strategy had failed and did the incredibly strenuous work of reversing the damage. I can't emphasize how rare that willingness to change, and admit error, is in business.

Most executives are very smart people. In thirty years of visiting corporate headquarters, I don't think I've ever met a single dumb person who had risen to helm a publicly traded company. But very few leaders, despite their intelligence, are willing to face hard facts and revise their thinking. That's one of the main reasons more businesses fail than succeed. The same thing is true in money management. You don't wind up running hundreds of millions or even billions of dollars of other peoples' money without being intelligent. But intelligence doesn't guarantee success. Peter Lynch, probably the most successful money manager in history, said the best you can hope for is to be right six times out of ten when it comes to picking winning companies.* Think about that for a second. The man most people credit as being one of the greatest, if not *the* greatest, investor

---

*Interview with Peter Lynch, *PBS Frontline,* January 14, 1997.

FLOWER POWER

Peter Lynch estimated that for every ten stocks he studied (and he studied just about every stock out there), he usually identified one worth buying. He also said that he only found a handful of truly great stocks in his entire career. Once he located those "five baggers" or "ten baggers," as he called his big winners, he held on to them. Unfortunately, not many investors follow this model. They see a stock they own start to go up and they panic that it might have hit its peak, so they unload it.

I've already talked about the terrible habit of averaging down—buying a stock as it drops. That comes directly from an allergic reaction to the idea of failure. Investors don't want to admit they made a losing decision, so instead of cutting their losses and getting out, they actually double up and triple up on it. Selling a great stock too quickly is the opposite of averaging down, but it is also rooted in people's fear of failure; they'd rather take a small profit on an investment than risk it going down again. Lynch called these two mistakes, which often go together, "watering the weeds and cutting out the flowers."*

_____
*Peter Lynch interview.

we've ever seen readily admitted that he was wrong almost as much as he was right!

I've said it once, I'll say it again: if you want to be a good investor, learn to be a good quitter. Quit early and quit often. And you might as well make friends with the feeling of disappointment, because it's certainly going to make friends with you. No matter how smart or savvy you are, if you play the markets, you're going to spend some up-close-and-personal time with your own fallibility, because failure in the stock market happens all the time—even to the most accomplished professional money managers in the financial industry. And yet, just like in the corporate world, most investors refuse to acknowledge this inescapable reality. That denial leads to some all-too-common mistakes.

EIGHT

LOSING MONEY WITHOUT EVEN TRYING

Welcome to Wall Street

It is difficult to get a man to understand something when his salary depends upon his not understanding it.

—Upton Sinclair

The only trouble with capitalism is the capitalists—they're too damn greedy.

—Herbert Hoover

MY IMMEDIATE SUPERVISOR AT MY FIRST JOB IN FINANCE at Texas Commerce Bank was the trust department's senior portfolio manager, a tall, lanky Michigan native who answered directly to Geoff Raymond. He was and still is one of the most trusting and warm-hearted people I have ever met. Unfortunately, those qualities are not terribly helpful in the money management game. If anything, they can get you into trouble. They certainly did in his case.

One morning early in my time in Houston, he strolled over to my cubicle and told me he was strongly considering buying large stakes in two stock offerings. One was a secondary offering for a restaurant management company that owned a bunch of Shoney's restaurant franchises. The other was an initial offering for a new subsidiary of the First National Bank and Trust Company of Oklahoma City. The bank planned to spin off its data-processing unit into a separate entity called First Data Management Company (stock symbol: FDMC) so that it could, theoretically, sell its services to smaller banks in the region. My boss asked me to look through the prospectuses of the two companies, do some due diligence, and write up a standard, two-page report on each of them, as required by our bank's compliance department.

The restaurant company took almost no time to vet. Shoney's restaurants were hugely popular at the time all over the South, so I could see no reason not to recommend that stock. First Data Management was another story. When I looked through its projections, it was obvious that most of its revenue was going to come from the First National Bank and Trust of Oklahoma City—the same company that was making it into a separate entity. It just seemed weird. Why go through the trouble of spinning off one of your units when all it was going to do was turn around and perform the same services for you it had always performed? Since I was no expert on the world of interbank data processing, I called the executive who ran Texas Commerce's own data-processing section and put the question to him. He was as perplexed as I was.

"I don't get it either, Scott," he said. "I wish I could help you. Good luck."

I spent the next couple of hours trying to make the numbers make sense, but I simply couldn't see a good reason why the bank was forming this subsidiary. It wasn't until I called the executive in charge of data processing for my bank's biggest competitor in Houston, a bank called First City, that I started to get an inkling of what the bank in Oklahoma was up to.

"It definitely seems fishy," the man said. "It's not like there's a huge market for other banks to pay for that service. And you know, a lot of people don't think First National is going to last much longer. They made all kinds of bad loans during the oil boom."

You may recall that loads of banks back then had been "lending on iron," meaning they gave out loans to energy companies using oil drilling equipment as collateral. After the price of oil crashed, almost all of those loans went bad and the "iron" used to back them up was virtually worthless. First National, like just about every other bank in the region (including my own, as I was soon to find out), was in desperate need of a cash infusion. Suddenly, its mysterious plan to spin off its data-processing service seemed a lot less mysterious. The company stood to make millions on the offering.

The third phone call I made that day was to the brokerage handling the stock offering, Montgomery Securities in San Francisco. The institutional salesman there who had recommended the stock was named Rick. Like just about everybody else at Montgomery, Rick was an aggressive pitchman. The word *bulldog* gets thrown around a lot, but I don't think that quite captures the level of mindless tenacity the brokers at Montgomery brought to their work. Picture an angry hyena that hasn't eaten in a couple of days. Now picture someone throwing a bloody porterhouse in front of it. That's how hard these guys sold their deals.

After I introduced myself, I told Rick about the research I had done and informed him as courteously as I could that I would not be recommending the stock.

"The bank is on the verge of insolvency," I explained. "If they're this new company's main customer, that's not going to be good for their earnings or their share price."

Rick barked into the phone, "How old are you, kid?"

I swallowed hard and replied, "Twenty-five."

"You've got a lot to learn," Rick growled. "Nobody stops me from collecting a commission. I'm not going to waste my time talking to you. I'll call your boss first thing in the morning."

The line went dead. I stared at the receiver in disbelief. I didn't understand what had just happened. I had informed a representative of a prestigious, well-respected brokerage that a stock they were offering had significant downside risk. I had assumed that he would be grateful for my insights, or at least interested in what I had to say. Instead, he had acted like I had belched in his ear.

In reality, Rick was right: I did have a lot to learn. The idea that someone on Wall Street would give a damn about the truth or doing the right thing by his clients was almost laughably naive.

True to his word, Rick did call my supervisor first thing in the morning and convinced him to buy $2 million worth of First Data Management's IPO for our trust accounts. Needless to say, the stock did not perform well. Two years after my phone call to Rick, First National was seized by the government. With its main customer insolvent, First Data Management scraped by for a little while longer before it was bought out by a larger competitor for a fraction of its IPO value.

My boss was not a bad money manager. Far from it. When I showed up at Texas Commerce, he had an outstanding investment record. Unlike most of the fund managers in Texas at the time, he had stayed clear of energy stocks during the oil mania, so after the bust our funds significantly outperformed our competition. But for all of his talent, he also had a critical weakness: *he thought he had friends on Wall Street.*

After he brought me out to San Francisco with him to work at GT Capital, he bought into two more ill-fated stock offerings on the advice of another Wall Street "friend" at the brokerage Hambrecht & Quist. One was SHL Systemshouse (stock symbol: SBN). The other was Westwood One Radio (stock symbol: WON). Just like First Data Management, they both quickly crashed. The brass at GT Capital were not pleased.

My boss thought his friends were looking out for his best interests. The opposite was almost certainly true. They knew they were passing off garbage, and they called him because they knew that he might be trusting enough to take it off their hands. After almost three decades in this business, I can say one thing without reservation: people on Wall Street are not looking out for anybody's interest but their own, and they often take care of those interests by screwing someone else. Many are, by and large, very bad people. But my boss made an even bigger mistake than trusting the morals of his Wall Street pals: *he thought they possessed some kind of superior insight for picking stocks.*

Firms like Montgomery Securities and Hambrecht & Quist were famous for hiring the best and the brightest to work in their research departments—smart, highly ambitious go-getters from places like Princeton, Yale, and Stanford. The brokerages would vastly overpay these whiz kids to "analyze" the companies they were underwriting.

And by analyze, I mean they paid them to concoct impressive-sounding facts and figures for salesmen like Rick to use to convince fund managers that those companies were good investments. Sometimes, as with the Shoney's franchisor, this research actually turned out to be true. Just as often, if not more so, it was bogus. Take First Data Management. Here I was, a twenty-five-year-old greenhorn straight out of business school, and it only took me one afternoon to figure out that that stock was a likely loser. And yet, according to Montgomery's all-star analysts, it couldn't fail.

After thirty years of doing this, I can tell you in no uncertain terms that buying stocks on the word of so-called *experts* is the single biggest mistake an investor can make. If somebody tries to tell you that they know something special about a given stock or the wider financial markets, they're probably either (a) doing something illegal or (b) trying to scam you. Either way, you would be a fool to follow their advice. I'm not saying you should always ignore stock tips, even from untrustworthy sources like institutional salesmen. But you have to remember Ronald Reagan's famous adage—trust, but *verify*. My boss forgot that crucial second step. He let those salesmen schmooze him into believing that they knew something about those stocks that nobody else knew.

Money managers have wised up a great deal since the 1980s when it comes to relying on advice from broker-dealers like Montgomery. By and large, we've learned our lesson. But Wall Street still manages to find plenty of suckers. The entire country of Iceland went bankrupt in the late 2000s because a handful of bankers there committed the same mistake my immediate boss at Texas Commerce did: they picked up the phone when some institutional salesmen called with supposedly can't-miss deals. Of course, in that case, brokerages like Goldman Sachs and Lehman

DIM BULBS

You hear the phrase "the best and the brightest" all the time these days. But most people don't remember that it was originally meant as an ironic dig at the arrogance of our country's elites. It was the title of a book by David Halberstam about how Ivy League technocrats foolishly entangled us in the Vietnam War. In the years since Halberstam's book was published, the words have lost their original irony. They've become a *positive* way to describe the latest generations of privileged, mostly Ivy League–educated elites. Most of those kids go into finance now instead of government or public service—and they have made as big a mess of our financial system as their predecessors did in Southeast Asia.

Brothers were peddling billions in subprime mortgage bonds instead of a couple million in some cash-strapped bank in Oklahoma. But the results were the same. Like my old supervisor, the bankers chose to believe that Wall Street experts had devised new, sophisticated methods for beating the markets—and the whole country went to zero because of it.

This misplaced faith in Wall Street whizzes is a symptom of a much larger and more destructive problem in the investment world: the cult of the guru. Investors of all types—from fund managers to day traders to mom-and-pop savers hoping to boost their 401(k) accounts—are constantly looking for a market messiah, someone who's figured out—once and for all—the magical formula for how to beat the Street. It is an understandable but self-defeating desire, because *the people who actually possess these kinds of insights almost never share them.* Think about it. Why would someone who has discovered an edge destroy its profitability by telling the world about it? And yet a never-ending cavalcade of self-promoters is able to convince people that they have an easy path to market riches.

All my life, I've watched these types rise and fall. When I was a kid, a guy named Joe Granville was famous for giving his presentations with a parrot on his shoulder. In the eighties, Robert Prechter showed up on the scene with all sorts of charts and graphs and trend lines talking about Elliot Waves and Kondratieff Curves. Both these guys made fortunes selling newsletters and speaking at conferences. Granville once declared that he could use his system to predict earthquakes. He even named a time and date when Los Angeles would break off into the Pacific Ocean. Thankfully, he was as good at calling Armageddon as he was at picking stocks.

Then there was Elaine Garzarelli, a hotshot young analyst at Shearson Lehman Brothers who became an instant star after she predicted the Black Monday stock market crash of 1987. She went on to make regular appearances as a commentator on television and even starred in a commercial for pantyhose. Her bosses were so eager to believe that they had found a once-in-a-lifetime genius, they handed her control of a giant mutual fund. A few years later, they had to fire her. She'd lost untold millions. In his book *The Fortune Sellers,* William A. Sherden analyzed her performance during the decade following the crash and found that she had correctly predicted the market all of 38 percent of the time.* As

---

*William A. Sherden, *The Fortune Sellers* (San Francisco: Wiley, 1999), 6.

Sherden pointed out, for all of her supposedly sophisticated analysis and widely acclaimed acumen, Garzarelli would have made better forecasts if she'd just flipped a coin. She may have called the crash of '87 and she may have been a charming guest on talk shows, but like so many other stock market celebrities, her actual investment record was abysmal.

I could go on and on listing these types. There is never a shortage of them. After Garzarelli, there was the much ballyhooed Jack Grubman. During the dotcom mania, Salomon Smith Barney paid him $20 million a year for his analysis of the telecom sector. Much of this analysis involved praise for companies that were paying Salomon huge amounts of money for banking services. My favorite quote from Grubman was when he said that being objective was another word for being uninformed.* After the crash, we all learned just how little he cared for objectivity. One of the companies he hyped the hardest was WorldCom, which turned out to be a colossal fraud. Salomon later admitted to doling out special shares of hot tech IPOs to WorldCom executives.†

Unfortunately, even after this *decades*-long parade of one discredited expert after another, the cult of the guru is still going strong. All you have to do is turn on the television today or spend a few minutes on the internet, and you'll see the latest generation of Granvilles and Prechters, Garzarellis and Grubmans.

---

*Amy Feldman and Joan Caplin, "Is Jack Grubman the Worst Analyst Ever?" *Money Magazine,* April 5, 2002.

†Charles Gasparino, "Salomon Admits That It Sent Hot IPOs WorldCom's Way," *Wall Street Journal,* August 27, 2002.

THE MOST DANGEROUS
PEOPLE IN THE WORLD

The financial world suffers from an inherent flaw: the people who work in it, by and large, are terrible investors.

Number one: *They've spent their whole lives going along to get along.* They're climbers, strivers, joiners, cheerleaders. (That's how they got those good degrees and those prestigious jobs in the first place!) This makes them naturally prone to groupthink and all too susceptible to manias and asset bubbles.

Number two: *They are hypercompetitive,* which keeps them from admitting failure and adjusting their strategies when things inevitably go wrong. This makes them all too susceptible to disastrous behaviors like averaging down and clinging to bad ideas.

Number three: *They worship rich and powerful people,* so they automatically defer to authority instead of questioning popular assumptions. Again, this makes them susceptible to manias and asset bubbles. It also creates an even more destructive mind-set—once they themselves rise to positions of power, they see *themselves* as infallible and worthy of worship.

Add it all up and there's only one conclusion you can reach: these are the last people you want safeguarding your money. And it's not just me saying this. The numbers back me up. The great author and investor John Bogle—who invented the passive index fund back in the 1970s—examined the average returns of equity mutual funds from 1983 to 2003. A dollar invested in those kinds of funds in the early 1980s netted just $7.10 in profits twenty years later. Over the same period, a dollar invested in the S&P 500 index, which Bogle's Vanguard 500 Fund tracks, would have brought in over $11.50.*

Think about those numbers for a second. The overseers of the Vanguard 500 merely invest in all the stocks of the S&P 500. Compare that to your average mutual fund, where you've got highly paid professional investors buying and selling individual stocks all day, every day. (And when I say highly paid, I mean it. Bogle has calculated the total fees and commissions reaped by the financial industry at more than $500 *billion* a year.) For all that extra effort, and all that extra expense, all of those well-compensated experts earned considerably less than an index fund whose managers did next to nothing.

Not all money managers are doomed to eternal underperformance, just most of them. A handful beat the market consistently, even after all taxes and fees. Warren Buffet comes to mind. Peter Lynch, too. Not to brag or put myself in those guys' class, but I think my twenty-three-year record as a hedge fund manager is also proof that the indexes *are* beatable. But finding someone who can do it for you year in and year out is next to impossible. While frauds mug for publicity on cable television, the really gifted money managers almost always go out of their way to avoid attention. Even if you can track them down, good luck convincing them to take your money. Most of them already have more than enough clients and, as I'll discuss shortly, they know the dangers of growing their assets too large.

---

*John Bogle, "The Mutual Fund Industry 60 Years Later: For Better or Worse?," *Financial Analyst Journal* 61, no. 1 (2005): 15–24.

I don't know how else to put this, so I'll just be blunt: *If you are an individual investor, you should not under any circumstances trust your money to a Wall Street brokerage or investment management company.* The vast majority of people in my business have the wrong temperaments for investing. So unless you are uniquely positioned to find that rare manager who can outperform the market over the long term, do what John Bogle has been urging people to do for decades: put your money in an index fund and leave it there. You'll make more, and you'll pay less in fees to do it.

The attributes I listed earlier—joinerism, power worship, hypercompetitiveness, intellectual torpor—lead to some very common investment mistakes like averaging down and trusting the word of so-called experts. Worst of all, though, those qualities also cause far too many money managers to confuse success with the size of their assets. They think bigger is always better—and they screw their clients out of higher returns because of it.

Back when I was in business school in the early 1980s, the big idea in economics was something called the efficient markets hypothesis. It was formed by University of Chicago professor Eugene Fama. To simplify it as much as possible, Fama said that all stocks are efficiently priced at all times. In other words, the collective wisdom of the marketplace correctly sets the value of all publicly traded companies. In general, I agree. I think the stocks of most companies *are* efficiently priced. That's why I believe average investors should only put their money into index funds—period, full stop. However, during my time at Texas Commerce Bank in Houston and even more so afterward, I began to suspect a possibly lucrative flaw in Fama's thesis.

Early in my career, I noticed that the stocks of smaller companies are *not* always efficiently priced. The reason is relatively simple: most people in the financial industry ignore these smaller companies, and it's awfully hard for the market to be efficient in pricing a stock if there's no market to speak of for that stock. I exploited this fact to earn outsized returns back when I was running mutual funds for GT Capital, and I've continued to make profits as a hedge fund manager by taking advantage of it. But very few of my peers follow this strategy. You might wonder why. The answer is that they're too greedy and vain to do so.

Most financial professionals can't resist maximizing the amount of money they have under their control. The more assets they bring into their funds, the more they make in fees. They also get the ego boost of putting a "b" instead of an "m" in front of the "-illions" they manage. I can't fault them too much. Who doesn't want to make more money? But by sucking so many assets in the door, as the saying goes, they inevitably wind up limiting their own performance potential, thus shrinking the amount they earn for their investors. You might call it the asset-size paradox. It's a fixed, if seldom discussed, rule of money management: *Asset size is the enemy of return.* The bigger you get, the lower your returns. That might sound contradictory, but it's really a simple matter of liquidity and price efficiency.

If you've got billions upon billions of dollars to manage, there's no way you can invest in those smaller, less-efficiently priced stocks that defy Fama's theory. There just aren't enough of them out there to handle that kind of volume. The only options for deploying such massive pools of money are giant, well-known companies with huge market capitalizations. But—of course—everyone else and their uncle and their uncle's friend Sal is already studying and evaluating and investing in those kinds of companies, too. That means there's no way to profit from inefficiencies in price because there are no inefficiencies in price. As usual, there's an old investment saying to capture this problem: when the microscopes come out, returns get microscopic.

The best example of the asset-size paradox is probably Julian Robertson and his legendary Tiger Management Hedge Fund. The fund's performance was phenomenal when it was still well under $1 billion. But Robertson kept pulling in more and more assets—the minimum investment in Tiger increased to a cool $5 million—and as the fund got more bloated, it started to act more like an overfed housecat than a tiger. In its last years, Robertson's fund lost enormous amounts of money, including a reported $2 billion in a single day in 1998.* By the time it shut down in 2000, Tiger may well have lost more money in total than it had made. Interestingly, the fund's CAGR (compound annual growth rate) was strongly positive over the course of its existence. Robertson biographer Daniel Strachman puts the figure at 31.7 percent.† But because he managed much larger amounts during the fund's final few years, which were also its *worst* years, Robertson's record in actual dollar amounts is much less impressive. Famed short-seller John Paulson suffered a similar fate. He made billions for himself and his investors by shorting the real estate market in 2008 and 2009. But after his assets exploded to the massive size of over $20 billion, he quickly stopped looking like a genius. His funds lost half their value in the single year of 2011, and they continued to slide in 2012.

When I was at GT Capital, I told my bosses I didn't want to make this mistake. I warned them that if they kept bringing in new investors,

---

*"Tiger Slain as Losses Plunge Hedge Fund into the Red," CNN.com, November 2, 1998.

†Daniel A. Strachman, *A Tiger in the Land of Bulls and Bears* (San Francisco: Wiley, 2004), 169.

my returns would drop. But they refused to listen. I knew my situation was hopeless when I found out they had hired a legendary boiler room brokerage in Denver to market my funds. The place's name was Blinder, Robinson but everybody called them "Blind 'em and Rob 'em." They were a western version of old-school penny promoters like First Jersey Securities or the now-famous Wolf of Wall Street's Stratton Oakmont, and they made their money the same way—by hawking dubious stocks to gullible investors. As soon as I learned that the higher-ups at GT had contracted with such a sleazy outfit, I immediately started looking for another job. It was abundantly clear to me that GT, like every other Wall Street firm, was only interested in vacuuming up as many assets as they could, even if it meant hurting their own customers.

The things I've been talking about in this chapter are not foreign to most people in my industry. Far from it. They're the worst-kept secrets in the financial world. Deep down, everybody knows that, just like corporations, more investments fail than succeed. Deep down, everybody knows that Wall Street brokerages routinely push bad investments to maximize their profits. And, deep down, everybody knows that overgrowing assets is bad for performance.

To borrow a phrase, these are inconvenient truths for my business. We all know them, yet most of us desperately try to pretend that we don't. But that doesn't mean they're not real or that they don't have very real consequences—and not just for individual investors or people in the investment business. These inconvenient truths are bad for our whole society.

Think about how bigger assets hurt performance. It's no wonder nobody in the financial world wants to admit this. Doing so would not only cost them money, it would force them to admit an even larger, more inconvenient truth: unlike the best companies in the private sector, Wall

Street often produces products that *cannot scale.* Let me explain what I mean. Microsoft's Windows operating system or Amazon's online book-selling platform are massively scalable inventions. The more customers they reach, the more profits they bring in, without sacrificing any of the quality they give to the consumers who use them. Conversely, the more customers Wall Street firms bring in to their investment vehicles, the poorer those products perform. Imagine if that happened with a new smartphone. As more people bought the phone, the quality of its service declined. How long do you think the company producing that phone would survive? And yet, year after year, Big Finance continues to reap massive profits—not for its clients, of course, but for itself.

The asset-size paradox isn't the only thing that separates Wall Street from the rest of the private sector. Can you think of another business in the world that would continue to exist as a going concern even after it had been proven definitively—as John Bogle of Vanguard proved about the financial industry—that most of its products are vastly inferior to other, cheaper alternatives like index funds? I can't. How about a business whose most prestigious firms have been caught defrauding their own customers not once, but over and over again? In the normal corporate world, would such a business not only continue to operate, but actually make more and more money every year? Of course not. It would be long dead by now. And yet *deceiving its clients and foisting inferior and even fraudulent products on them is exactly how Wall Street stays in business!*

HEDGED

After all my talk of Wall Street types making poor investors, you might think I would keep my money strictly in index funds. But that's not case.

I'm proud to say that, unlike some of my peers in the business, I keep almost all of my money in my own hedge fund. I've also made a practice of putting a little bit into other hedge funds, as well, usually ones that are just starting out. I know what it's like trying to get a new venture off the ground, so I like to help people out. Some of these newcomers wind up earning great returns for me. Others, not so much.

In 2005, I invested $100,000 with someone who lived near me and went to the same church I (occasionally) attend. He seemed like a smart, straight-shooting guy. He was affable and confident in his abilities, so I figured, Why not give him a chance and see what he could do?

It turned out what he could do was separate me from my money.

I'd always heard about the sleazy tricks fund managers use to fleece their investors. But I'd never been on the business end of any of them personally until I signed over that money to my former friend.

The first thing that worried me was that he bought a lot of dodgy green energy companies brought public by an investment bank run by a Silicon Valley promoter named Laird Cagan. We're talking about pure "story" stocks, companies whose only assets were a couple of engineering PhDs and—maybe—a patent or two. To be honest, I was ready to write my investment off when I saw those stocks in the audited financials. But to my pleasant surprise, my friend's picks actually did pretty well. By early 2008, only a couple years after I'd signed over my 100K to him, my stake had more than tripled, at least on paper.

I met up with my friend that summer, and I told him that while I was thrilled with his performance so far, I didn't feel good about the direction of the markets. This was a few months after Bear Stearns had crashed and burned. Things were getting dire, and I urged him to start shorting stocks, something he had always been reluctant to do.

"You're running a hedge fund," I said. "Now's the time to start hedging."

He gave me a bashful smile and shook his head. "You're right—the markets are looking iffy, Scott," he said. "But, trust me, we've done our homework. The companies we own are going to keep going up even if everything else crashes."

You can probably guess how I reacted to his optimistic prediction. The next day, I wrote him an email requesting a $150,000 redemption. With the way things were looking in those days, what I really wanted to do was take everything out of his fund and put it under the nearest mattress. But I figured withdrawing that much would at least allow me to get my money back, plus a nice 50 percent return. As for the rest, I was ready to sacrifice it on the altar of my friend's naiveté. That is, until he had the nerve to refuse my redemption request.

After not hearing from him for an entire week following my first email, I wrote him by snail mail with my banking details and instructions for wiring the money. Two days later, a letter arrived in the mail—and what a letter it was. My friend's fund was quite small as far as hedge funds go. He only had about $7 million under management. But what he lacked in size, he made up for in chutzpah.

"As you know," he wrote, "the timing of making a distribution to you is a function of complying with the appropriate ratio of retirement funds to non-retirement funds in the fund—no more than twenty-five percent of the fund can be invested in retirement accounts. Since we are very close to this ratio, I will have to attract new investors that are non-retirement accounts in order to maintain the proper ratio before I can make a distribution to you."

If you've never invested in a hedge fund, or at least tried to pull your money out of one, this passage probably sounds like a bunch of nonsense. That's because it is. Like a lot of hedge fund managers, my friend had placed an absurdly long ninety-day waiting period on redemptions. But even that was not enough for him. Even with three months' notice,

---

SPIKED

In 2010, the owner of the Cleveland Browns tried to take his money out of a hedge fund, only to be told that a provision in his investment contract prevented redemptions that amounted to more than 20 percent of the fund's assets. That was a serious problem because, as it turned out, he was the *only* investor in the fund! So, according to that provision, because the managers of the fund had done such a poor job of attracting other investors, the Browns owner was obligated to keep his money in their hands . . . *forever!*

No, Franz Kafka did not come back from the dead and go into the investment business. This was a fund managed by a perfectly respectable husband-and-wife team with Ivy League degrees and extensive experience in the financial world.* Unfortunately, those kinds of credentials do not guarantee success or integrity. The Browns owner sued the couple, and a judge ordered the return of his investment.

---

*Peg Brickley, "Cleveland Browns Owner on Offense Against Hedge Fund," *Wall Street Journal,* March 8, 2011.

he still couldn't or simply didn't want to come up with my money, so he concocted this bunkum about maintaining a percentage of retirement accounts under management. Unfortunately, this has become standard practice in my industry. It's shocking how many hedge funds "gate" their investors by inventing all kinds of legalese excuses to refuse redemptions.

In his letter to me, my former friend not only politely refused to give me back my own money, he also served notice that, if and when he did get around to giving it back to me, he was planning to do so, at least in part, in the form of securities. Now, that might have been acceptable if he were talking about shares of easily tradable companies like AT&T or Intel. But as I've already said, my friend owned some pretty sketchy stocks—and a lot of them were about as liquid as Death Valley in the middle of July. I sent him a very blunt email informing him that I was not going to be pleased if he gave me stocks instead of cash. So, what did he do? He stuck me with a bunch of illiquid positions—specifically, over ten thousand "legend" shares of a company known at the time as AE Biofuels (stock symbol: AEBF).

If you don't know what legend shares are, they are stocks given or sold to insiders, and they almost always come with restrictions on when or how they can be sold. The AE Biofuels shares my friend gave me weren't allowed to be traded until late December of that year. So not only did I have to wait three months to get my money out of his fund, I then had to wait *another* three months to turn the shares he gave me into cash. I was so angry about getting a bunch of unsellable stock, I immediately demanded another $100,000 from him. This time, he responded with ten thousand in cash and another 19,400 legend shares of, you guessed it,

AE Biofuels. That meant I now owned a total of 30,114 shares of more or less worthless pieces of paper.

Here's the thing about legend shares: companies are required to notify the public when a bunch of them are about to come onto the market, and the minute they do so, the stock price almost always crashes. When I received my first batch of AE Biofuels shares in September, they were trading for around $7. By early December, after I'd gotten the next slug of them, the price was down to $3.35. Then, on December 10, the company noted in an SEC filing that "a significant number" of legend shares were about to become eligible for sale. Not surprisingly, investors sold off AEBF in droves. By the time I was legally permitted to try to offload my holdings, the price was down to, get this, *42 cents!*

PERFORMANCE ENHANCEMENT

It hurts to lose tens of thousands of dollars. It hurts a lot, especially when my friend's own legally audited reports said I had actually *made* hundreds of thousands. But there are always risks when you make a new investment. And it's not like I can't afford to lose some money. I can. What galls me is how easy it was for him to screw me over and how routine this behavior is in the financial world.

There are countless tricks that brokers and money managers have mastered to pad their stats and separate their clients from their money. New ones get invented all the time. Back in the dotcom days, fund managers would stash hot IPO shares they'd get from brokerage houses into separate, personal accounts. More recently, managers have been paying top dollar for "research" from so-called expert networks of current and former employees at public companies—research that almost always includes blatant inside information on things like pending earnings reports. This is what got hedge fund manager Steven Cohen in trouble in 2013. It also brought down the multibillion-dollar Galleon Group fund in 2009.

The only limits on these kinds of shenanigans are the depths of shady managers' imaginations and the shallowness of their morals. In other words, there are no limits. We're talking about people who possess a very dangerous combination of character traits: they're intelligent, unscrupulous, and greedy. Not all of their schemes involve out-and-out theft or clearly illegal behavior. But they're still a long way from kosher.

One of the things that still gets me riled up about my experience with my former friend is that, to receive all those worthless AE Biofuels shares, I had to open up my own personal brokerage account. I still haven't sold them, and to this day they are the only stocks in that account. It just about makes me sick when I get my statements every month. You may be wondering why opening an account would be so upsetting for me, and why I haven't put any other stocks in there to offset those terrible AEBF shares. The answer is, it's a matter of principle. As I said, besides my occasional investment in other hedge funds, I keep almost all of my money in my own fund. I'm very proud of this fact, not only because it means I'm willing to risk my own wealth on the trades I make for my investors but because it shows that I'm not engaging in probably the oldest and most popular bit of legerdemain in my business: front running.

Imagine you're a money manager with a couple hundred million dollars of other people's capital at your disposal. Now imagine that you're planning to buy a large stake in Acme Incorporated, which is running $10 a share. You think it's going higher, so you decide you're going to put $5 million of your clients' money into it. But before you do that, you call up your own personal broker and you say, "I would like ten thousand shares of Acme Inc.," and then you wait until your own trade is done before you pull the trigger on behalf of your mutual fund or your hedge fund.

Now, a $5 million buy is inevitably going to bid up Acme Inc., at least in the short term. Maybe it'll only go up a couple cents if Acme happens to be a larger, more liquid concern. But if it's a less-frequently traded stock, that investment could lift the price as much as a few dollars. Whatever it is, you watch the tape until you figure that the bump from your fund's investment has maxed out, then you quietly call your personal broker again and tell him to unload your stake. Let's say in Acme's case, the stock rises one whole point before you cash out. Congratulations—you just made $10,000 in a matter of hours. And all you had to do for it was make a few phone calls.

Front running has been out of control for a long, long time—and nothing's changed. There are guys in my industry, guys I know personally, guys who are some of the most prominent citizens in the Bay Area, who have been front running for *decades*. The father-in-law of a prominent Northern California politician was an infamous front runner. It was probably the worst-kept secret in Marin County. Everybody knew he was pocketing hundreds of thousands, maybe even millions, by using his clients' funds to juice up his own trades. But nobody gave a damn.

Front running might seem like a victimless crime, but it's far from it. How can anyone be sure front runners are making the best trades for their investors? Who's to say they aren't buying stocks based on how susceptible they are to rising on a big buy order? They might actually be buying into terrible companies that have no chance of succeeding in the long run. If the stocks sink, why should a front runner care? They've already made their cut. And what about all the honest investors out there who are scouting stocks based on old-fashioned things like earnings and growth? If you've got fund managers out there jacking up share prices with millions of dollars in other peoples' capital purely for their own benefit, those metrics mean less and less. Pretty soon, the whole financial system gets warped. Money management isn't about finding quality investments anymore, it's all about short-term gains. And it's not about assessing and managing risk because there is no risk for a front runner! They're virtually guaranteed a profit. That's called a rigged game, and it's the exact opposite of what a fair and free market is supposed to be.

There is a more fundamental reason why I care about shady practices like front running in my industry. It has to do with simple fairness and professionalism. As money managers, our customers trust us with their livelihoods, the wealth they have built to sustain themselves and their families. We charge them enormous amounts of money in fees in exchange for the promise that we will do everything we can to safeguard that wealth and grow it as much as possible. But that's not what happens. It seems like more and more people in my business see their clients' money as a convenient pool of assets they can exploit to grow their *own* wealth. Even more shockingly, this attitude is not limited to individual fund managers. Like a bad video on the internet, it's gone viral and infected the entire system—even the biggest, most prestigious firms.

Have you ever wondered why so many mutual funds—and a good deal of hedge funds now, too—have a so-called family of funds? Seriously, take a look at the marketing materials for your average mutual fund company. It's probably got a catalog of funds longer than the wine list at the French Laundry (which, if you haven't had a chance to eat there, runs over a hundred pages). There's a good reason for this, and it stems from that old inconvenient truth about the financial industry: asset size is the enemy of return.

As companies bring in more and more investment capital, their performance inevitably declines. But do they stop taking on more assets? Of course not. They just start another fund and give it a catchy new name like their "Dynamic Growth Fund" or some such BS. As a smaller, leaner fund, this new entity has a chance to reap much larger returns. Fund managers often make sure this happens by transferring winning trades from larger funds to these newer, smaller ones. They then market the hell out of those newer funds by touting their astounding returns until those funds, too, get too big to keep posting great stats. Then, rinse and repeat—they start the whole cycle again.

But what about the new funds that *don't* do well? There are plenty of those. And companies have a sure-fire strategy for dealing with them: they shut them down and erase them from their books. It's called survivorship bias, and it happens all the time. A fund goes south and starts to post poor results, so the bosses step in and—bingo, bango—it goes down the Wall Street rabbit hole, never to be heard from again. They either wipe it out entirely or they merge it into other, better-performing funds. Of course, the investors in that fund don't get their money back or anything. Those losses aren't imaginary for them. But if you read the mutual fund company's marketing materials, it's like the fund that lost them their money never existed.

Hedge fund managers do this, too. They'll shut down money-losing funds, only to reopen them months or years later. This allows them to bypass high-water mark provisions in their investment agreements so that they can charge the standard 20 percent performance fee before they fully recoup prior-year losses. Another classic trick is to squirrel away bad

G(R)IFTED

The thing that really gets me about guys like my former friend the hedge fund manager, and way too many others in my industry, is that they present themselves as pillars of their communities while they're secretly scamming their investors. The only reason I trusted my friend with my money in the first place was that he came off as a decent family man. I assumed that someone who seemed so wholesome would manage my money responsibly. That assumption was wrong.

Another way sleazy money managers burnish their reputations is by spreading huge amounts of money around to charities and other worthy causes. That was one of Bernie Madoff's main MOs, and it worked for him for decades. No one wanted to believe that such a generous philanthropist was a complete fraud.

A few years ago, I attended a fund-raiser for a school I helped found for disabled kids. It's a great event that we throw every year. We always start off with a silent auction and then we bring on some entertainment. That year, both Dana Carvey and Robin Williams were scheduled to perform. Before the auction could even get started, the singer Sammy Hagar, of all people, jumped on stage and declared that he and his buddy Larry Goldfarb were each going to donate $50,000 right then and there so that we could skip the auction and go right to the show. Larry was a local hedge fund manager with a reputation for partying with rock stars like Hagar and writing out big checks to charities. The audience applauded wildly, and Larry came on stage to take a bow. We were all thrilled at his classy, selfless gesture . . . until we found out the money he gave the school wasn't exactly clean. In 2011, Larry was busted for dipping into his clients' funds to bankroll his own pet projects and investments, including stakes in real estate ventures and a record company (remember, he liked to hang out with rock stars).* Some of Larry's investments actually made large returns, but he neglected to share those profits with the people who had made them possible—his investors.

Laird Cagan, the investment banker who fed my former friend those iffy green energy stocks, is a big-time donor to charity, too. Thanks to his generosity, the soccer stadium at Stanford University is named after him. But at least one of his gifts hasn't worked out so well for the people who received it. In 2007, Laird gave $1 million in stock to his hometown of Portola Valley to help finance a new town center. What a guy, right? Wrong. It's hard to believe, but Laird pulled the same game on his city as his pal pulled on me. The stock was restricted, and the town couldn't legally sell it until 2012. By then, it was worth a grand total of $60,000.†

---

*"SEC Charges Bay Area Hedge Fund Manager with Misappropriating 'Side Pocketed' Assets," SEC press release, March 1, 2011.

†Bonnie Eslinger, "Portola Valley Wants to Dump Donated Stock After Watching It Lose $940,000 in Value Since 2007," *San Jose Mercury News,* July 19, 2012.

investments in larger accounts so they won't affect the returns as much as they would have in smaller vehicles. This practice was so common in my area of Marin County, people used to call it the 101 Allocation after the main freeway here. Fund managers would shove their losing investments into big institutional accounts and put their winners into smaller funds—often the ones they themselves and their friends and family had invested in. Then, as the saying went, they'd be out the door and on Highway 101 by 1:01 p.m.

Tricks like allocation and front running have been around for a long time, and they're still quite popular. You might think someone in the regulatory sector would, I don't know, *regulate* these behaviors. But agencies like the Securities and Exchange Commission (SEC) aren't just outmanned and outgunned by Wall Street; they've essentially abdicated their responsibilities for overseeing my industry. Sure, they make occasional headlines for busting a few blatantly bad actors like Larry Goldfarb and Bernie Madoff, but these cases are the proverbial exceptions that prove a rule. The vast majority of Wall Street's scams not only go unpunished, but many of them are allowed to continue out in the open without the faintest threat of prosecution.

About ten years ago, I got a voice mail from a woman working for a well-known and well-connected boutique brokerage in Arkansas. She said they were arranging a PIPE (private investment in public equity) for Stonepath Group Inc. (stock symbol: STG), a troubled freight forwarder. A PIPE is a last-ditch funding mechanism for failing companies in which batches of discounted shares are sold to big investors like hedge funds. They almost never save the companies from bankruptcy, but they often wind up lining the pockets of shady money managers. At the time, Stonepath's stock was trading for $3, but the woman said that if I bought into the PIPE scheduled for a week later, I could purchase shares at a significant discount. She concluded her message with an astonishing bit of doublespeak: "By listening to this voice mail, you are now in receipt of nonpublic information and are thus prohibited in trading on the company's stock. But if you do decide to use this information to your benefit, it is not our role nor is it in our interest to question your decision."

I couldn't believe what I had just heard. Here was a complete stranger leaving me inside information on my voice mail, then all but winking and nodding at me as she invited me to use it. Why would she do such a thing? *Because the entire PIPE process depends on guys in my position doing exactly what she was supposedly telling me not to do—using that inside information to make a fast profit.*

Here's how it works. Brokerages like the woman's employer call up hedge fund managers all over the country and invite them to participate in an upcoming PIPE. The fund managers immediately short the stock of the company involved. Then, a week or so later, when the PIPE occurs, they buy in at the discounted price and use those exact shares to cover their positions. It's the easiest money you can possibly make. The fact that it's completely and unquestionably *against the law* doesn't matter one scintilla to anyone involved—not to the brokerages arranging them, not to the money managers profiting from them, and, unfortunately, not even to the regulators who are supposed to stop them.

Over the years, I've received several invitations to profit on inside information during PIPE deals. But that voice mail from the woman in Arkansas was so egregious, I decided I had to do something about it. I got the contact info for an SEC lawyer from a friend of mine, and I called the guy from my room at the Hyatt in Monterey during the American Electronics Association Conference. When I told him about the message

I'd received and how rampant the PIPE scam had become, he wasn't at all surprised about it.

"We're aware that some people have been covering short positions on PIPE offerings," he said. I'm not sure, but it sounded like he stifled a yawn midsentence.

"Are you planning on doing something about it?" I asked.

The lawyer let out a sigh. "Look, I'm going to be straight-up with you. Do you know what I make every year?" Before I could hazard a guess, he gave me the answer: "A buck twenty-five."

"Okay, you make $125,000 a year. That's not exactly minimum wage."

"No, it's not. But the guys shorting these PIPE deals make millions."

"But your job is to regulate those guys and enforce the law."

"Sure it is. But when it comes to things like this, that's a lot harder than it seems. The investigation would take years. They'd hire ten different lawyers and fight me every step of the way. And in the end, we'd be lucky if they wound up paying a small fine."

"Let me just make sure I understand what you're telling me," I said. "I just informed you that I have a licensed broker on tape giving me inside information and practically begging me to use it, but you don't plan to pursue the matter?"

"No," he stated flatly. "I do not."

"So all these people breaking the law are just going to keep getting away with it?"

He paused for a moment before answering.

"Yes, Mr. Fearon. I'm afraid they are."

CONCLUSION

LEARNING TO LOVE FAILURE ALL OVER AGAIN

When plunder becomes a way of life for a group of men living together in society, they create for themselves in the course of time a legal system that authorizes it and a moral code that glorifies it.

—Frederic Bastiat

Only those who dare to fail greatly can ever achieve greatly.

—Robert F. Kennedy

IN MORE THAN TWO DECADES OF RUNNING MY HEDGE fund, 2009 was the only year we lost money. And I'm not talking about a little money, either. After producing a compound annual growth rate of 13 percent after all fees for the previous eighteen years, and outperforming the S&P 500 by an average of almost 5 percent a year during that time, we were down over 12 percent in 2009. All told, my fund lost over $36 million on short investments. For larger funds, that would be a relatively minor hit, but at the time, I was only managing $140 million, so my short losses wiped out almost a third of our assets! Luckily, our long investments offset some of that and we were "only" down a net of $17 million.

Why did this happen? Mostly, it was my own fault. I blew it. I shorted a number of companies that I expected to fall steeply and even go to zero. Instead, almost all of them wound up rising on the year. What led me to these calamitous investments? You could say that I made some of the same mistakes that I describe in this book. It hurts to admit, but I misread the conditions of the markets as badly as Chemtrak's CEO did when he told me his take-home cholesterol test would outsell home pregnancy detectors. And like Global Marine's CFO and his magical rig utilization number, I clung too tightly to my formula for investing and failed to adapt to unforeseen circumstances. By the time I realized how badly I had goofed, I was caught just as flatfooted in the face of these new realities as the brass at Blockbuster when they tried to save themselves by selling candy and popcorn.

In some ways, I got caught up in a kind of mania, too. Things looked so dire after the 2008 crash, virtually nobody in the popular press and the financial world thought the markets would recover. I willingly joined in with the bears because I believed wholeheartedly in a certain narrative: things were going to get worse. Back in the dotcom days, people like Women.com's CEO were blinded to any chance they could fail. A decade later, in 2009, I couldn't see a way the companies I had shorted *couldn't* fail. As I have talked about repeatedly throughout this book, that sort of hubris is a dangerous thing in business and in investing.

I was definitely my biggest enemy in 2009. But something else was happening that year, too. The markets were not behaving the way they had behaved for my entire career, and the normal functioning of the financial system had been distorted. The companies I shorted were textbook examples of terminally ill businesses, with vanishing revenues and crushing debts. I didn't think many of them would last until Christmas. If someone had predicted that not only would all of them still be solvent by the end of the year, but that many of their stocks would have tripled and even quadrupled in value, I would have referred that person to a psychiatrist. But that's exactly what happened.

The reason for this was simple: our country's political, corporate, and financial elites wanted it that way. Unlike previous recessions, which mainly hit the working and middle classes, this recession rocked America's investing class, the very people running Wall Street and Washington—the very people who had caused the downturn in the first place. They refused to admit that they had failed as badly as all of the failed companies I have described in this book. So instead of letting the stocks and bonds of almost every major investment bank, and many other debt-laden companies, go to zero, they protected themselves from the consequences of their own ineptitude by turning our stock market into the financial equivalent of professional wrestling.

First came the massive injections of taxpayer cash into the financial sector. A lot has been written about that boondoggle, so I won't go into too much detail on it other than to say that it was the largest and most brazen upward redistribution of wealth in the history of capitalism—and it was only the beginning. Next, the Fed yanked interest rates down to virtually zero. They're still there as I write this. This move hasn't gotten the press that the Wall Street bailouts did, but it might have been even more destructive. It punished the prudent to help the profligate. People who had done the right thing and put money into their savings lost out so that poorly managed corporations could refinance what should have been fatal debt loads. Doomed businesses were able to replace high-interest, fast-maturing bond issues with longer-term paper yielding a fraction of what they would have owed otherwise. Congress even sweetened the deal by giving some companies additional five-year tax "look-backs," which allowed them to recalculate previous returns and claim giant retroactive refunds. It all added up to one big nationwide, taxpayer-subsidized cooking of the corporate books.

Almost to a person, the executives who ran the failed businesses I detailed in this book were decent, well-meaning individuals who acted in good faith. They sincerely believed in what they were doing, but for one reason or another, things just went wrong for them—as they often do in a healthy market economy. Like I said in the introduction, the thing that has made our country such a great incubator of innovation is the freedom we have always given our businesspeople—not just the freedom to make ridiculous amounts of money thanks to good decisions, but the freedom to go spectacularly broke because of bad ones.

But now that crucial freedom is in peril. And I'm not just saying that because I lost a few million dollars on some short investments in 2009. I can afford to lose some money. And unlike far too many of my peers on Wall Street, I don't need to keep making more and more just to please my ego. But the way I lost that money was very disturbing to me. I understand that we went through a major crisis and that solutions enacted in the fog of such a dire emergency are not always ideal. But here's the problem: nothing has changed in the interim.

After Charles Ferguson received the Best Documentary Oscar in 2011 for his brilliant film *Inside Job,* he stepped to the podium and made a terse statement: "Three years after a horrific financial crisis caused by fraud," he said, "not a single financial executive has gone to jail."* The crowd in attendance cheered him. For a day or so afterward, Ferguson's point was discussed and debated in the news media. Then, once again, the whole subject petered out.

Thanks to Ferguson's film and numerous other investigations, we know what caused the financial crisis. Some of the most powerful figures in the financial industry knowingly defrauded millions of people and stole billions, perhaps trillions of dollars. These weren't honest business mistakes. This wasn't like some misguided entrepreneur trying to market home cholesterol kits or open a Cajun restaurant in Marin County. Like Ferguson said, this was massive fraud. These were malicious, premeditated *crimes*. And yet the criminals who perpetrated them have never been held responsible. Incredibly, they were even rewarded for their misdeeds—not just with the massive bailouts that most people have heard about, but with the less publicized interventions that followed.

It's no secret why these powerful financial criminals were allowed to get away with the equivalent of an economic massacre. Again, as Ferguson and other brave journalists have documented, Wall Street has essentially *captured* the very systems that are supposed to monitor and police it. The SEC is a joke. Washington, DC, is essentially a one-party town now—the money party. The business media, with a few exceptions, is full of card-carrying Wall Street apologists. Even academia has been co-opted.

Every year I go back to Evanston, Illinois, and give a talk to the students of Northwestern's Kellogg School of Management, my graduate school alma mater. During a meet-and-greet event there in 2011, I found myself standing next to the new dean of the school and decided it was a

---

*"'Inside Job' Director Slams Wall Street," *Marketwatch*, February 28, 2011.

perfect opportunity to bring up an idea I'd had on the plane ride out from California. Just a few weeks earlier, Citibank had agreed to pay almost $300 million for knowingly selling its clients toxic subprime mortgage bonds. The year before, Goldman Sachs had paid the largest fine in history, $550 million, for engineering similar deals.

"Why don't you ban Citi and Goldman from recruiting at Kellogg for three years?" I suggested to the new dean.

She nearly spit up her drink. "Excuse me?" she asked with a nervous smile.

"They blatantly scammed their own clients," I went on. "They shouldn't have access to your students."

After a very awkward moment of silence, the dean patted me on the shoulder and stepped away into the crowd. "Nice talking to you, Scott," she said as she passed me by.

In retrospect, it was probably unfair of me to put the dean on the spot like that. She'd only taken the job a few months earlier. Even if she had liked my idea, I'm sure she wasn't anxious to take such a radical step so early in her tenure. But the fact remains that Wall Street essentially *owns* business education now, and it continues to buy off academics and universities by hiring graduates, awarding professors lucrative consulting jobs, and sponsoring seminars. As if to hammer this point home, when I flew back to the Bay Area the day after chatting with the new dean at Kellogg, the top letter on the stack of mail waiting for me in my office was an invitation to "The First Annual Goldman Sachs Global Education Conference" down at Stanford, my undergraduate alma mater.

They say that the cover-up is often worse than the crime. And the measures our government took in the wake of the crisis have amounted to a giant, ongoing cover-up that may have done more damage to our financial system than the original crimes. We as a society and our government had a chance to live up to our free-market principles; unfortunately, we torched them instead. Rather than sending the banks into receivership and breaking them up, we poured vast amounts of money into them, which has only made them bigger and less accountable than ever. Then by slashing rates and keeping them near zero for years on end, we've killed any incentive to save and created a kind of undead corporate culture with hundreds of zombie businesses still limping along that, in a truly free market, would have gone through bankruptcy long ago. This is not how prosperous economies function.

Most unconscionably, in my opinion, the government also rescued the bondholders of failed financial institutions like Washington Mutual (WaMu). These bondholders were not mom-and-pop investors. They were sophisticated institutional investors who knew the risks they were taking in purchasing those debt securities. Incredibly, former Treasury secretary Henry Paulson wrote in his book *On the Brink* that when WaMu was seized and sold to J. P. Morgan, he wanted to give its bond investors even *more* taxpayer money—up to one hundred cents on the dollar as opposed to the far lower amounts the bonds had been trading for the day the bank was seized. Paulson claimed he was seeking to allay "uncertainty" in the markets.* I've read that paragraph in Paulson's book over and over again (it's on page 293 in my copy), and it still astounds me. I don't think he is a bad person for holding these opinions. I just think he is profoundly wrong. Bailing out politically connected bondholders while millions of struggling homeowners got nothing wasn't just unfair, it was destructively unfair.

---

*Henry Paulson, *On the Brink* (New York: Business Plus, 2010), 293.

We heard a lot of talk about "moral hazard" during and after the financial crisis. But I don't think people really understand what that phrase means, or at least how truly dangerous it is. If you prevent failing businesses from restructuring—not just small businesses, but large and important businesses as well—then the managements of those firms lose any incentive to make smart, prudent decisions. They know they can take all the risk they want because they'll never have to suffer the consequences. That's bad enough. But moral hazard has had an even more pernicious effect than corrupting the behavior of our business leaders. It has corrupted the very purpose of our financial system.

In a healthy economy, capital markets fuel growth by allocating resources to smart ideas and well-run companies while starving out less-deserving ventures. But by protecting investors in the stocks and especially the bonds of failed companies, we've warped that process. Capital increasingly flows to politically favored businesses instead of innovative and well-managed concerns. That's not a free market; it's crony capitalism—a surefire way to hamper growth, job creation, and economic vitality.

I know it sounds contradictory, but I believe that if we want to return to a growing and dynamic economy, we have to learn to embrace failure again. We have to let the markets get back to their normal function of elevating good ideas and eliminating bad ones. I'm not saying this book can single-handedly accomplish this or undo the damage that's been done. But I hope it will help change people's perceptions of what creates growth and a healthy financial sector. I want to take away the stigma of failure. It's nothing to be ashamed or afraid of. If anything, we should celebrate the people who are brave enough to risk everything, even if they fall short. They're part of a long, rich tradition in this country. And our future prosperity depends on carrying on that tradition.

ACKNOWLEDGMENTS

FOUR YEARS AGO I GAVE A TALK TO A CLASS OF GRADUATE students at UC Berkeley's School of Journalism on unethical behavior in the money management world. After class, I told Lowell Bergman, the course professor, that I wanted to write a book about my investment adventures. A week later, journalism fellow Matt Issacs introduced me to his friend Jesse Powell, who agreed to help me out. And so our book-writing adventure began. Over the ensuing months and then years, Jesse and I met nearly one hundred times and hammered out every word of every sentence. As the work evolved, my father and two friends of mine, Mike Wilkins and Professor Robert Korajczyk of Northwestern's Kellogg School of Management, read early drafts and gave insightful feedback. Once the book was "in the can," we started searching for an agent and a publisher. With the help of Mickey Butts, we were lucky to find Elizabeth Kaplan, who directed the book to Palgrave Macmillan. Without Jesse, Elizabeth, and my editor, Emily Carleton, this book would never have been published. I am eternally thankful to all of them.

This book was also made possible by the many friends, analysts, and money managers who have helped me during the last three decades. My own analysts, former and current, set up many of the meetings described herein. Marty Carrade, Jeff Edman, Paul Flather, Brian Freckman, Pat Gaynor, Ben Sandler, and Mike Weil arranged a good number of these interviews. All had helpful insights, which we often debated at watering holes afterward. Other money managers attended meetings as well. These included Carlo Cannell, Fred Clark, Carter Dunlap, Mark Friedman, Dan Mendoza, Georgina Russell, Craig Stephens, and Greg Wettersten in California and Rob Alpert, Blair Baker, John Myers, Reid Walker, Wilson Jaeggli, and Nelson Jaeggli in Texas. Their questions and insights improved my decision-making ability. I am grateful for their help and thankful for their friendship. I also relied on consultants for identifying companies to visit. Wyatt Carr, Scott Cummings, Bill Fellows, Bryan Luter, and Chris Mooney are friends who enjoy interviewing managements almost more than I do. Their help has been invaluable.

The staff at Banyan Securities, where I sublease office space, have always been helpful and fun to talk with through the years. Gary Smith and Dick Banakus helped me set up my hedge fund. They, along with Dan Gressel, were also my first investors. Other investors on day one were Shelly Wolk, Larry Levitt, John Tomlin, Bob LeDoux, and Andre Robert. Amazingly, all still have money in my fund. I am grateful for the faith they, and all of my investors, have placed in me. Big thank-yous also go to my trader, Wendy Gee, and my administrative assistant, Cathy Pozo. Their tireless work and dependability has made my job and life much easier.

I would also like to thank my family—my parents; my brother Rick; my wife Jennifer; and my kids, Michael, Caroline, and Nicholas—all of whom bring me happiness and make my work easier through their support. While not discussed in this book, my life and life's focus changed dramatically on March 4, 1994, when my twins, Caroline and Nicholas, were born. Caroline, like her older brother, Michael, is a smart, kind, and confident young adult. But Nicholas has presented us with more than the usual challenges. At four months old, he was diagnosed with cystic fibrosis. By age three, he was diagnosed with moderate to severe autism. In his teens, Nicholas became epileptic. Thankfully, we have been able to stop his grand mal seizures with medication. While barely verbal, Nicholas laughs endlessly and finds happiness in simple activities like eating ice cream, watching Disney videos, and playing in hot tubs. I think I have helped Nicholas be happy and learn life skills. I know I have learned much from him. He has taught me patience, compassion, and the satisfaction that can be found from helping people who at times cannot help themselves. Everyone who works with Nicholas, from his home aides to his doctors at the University of California San Francisco Medical Center, has been amazing. Thank you.

Because of Nicholas, our family has become involved with charities that help the disabled. My wife and I started a school for autistic kids. We have thirty-seven students today, and I have been a board member for over a decade. One hundred percent of all profits I earn from this book will be donated to these charities.

Last, I am thankful I was born in America and grateful for the front-row vantage on its dynamic private sector that I have enjoyed. Despite its faults, this country remains a truly exceptional experiment in human history. Our nation's companies, big and small, its workforce, and its incredible entrepreneurs have made our economic engine the eighth wonder of the modern world.

INDEX